TO GREAT MEADOWS
WILDLIFE REFUG

N

MW00424139

W

S

62

SLEEPY HOLLOW
CEMETERY
AUTHORS' RIDGE

BEDFORD ST.

OLD HILL
BURYING
GROUND

STREET

ROAD

HAWTHORNE LANE

LEXINGTON   STREET

CAMBRIDGE   TURNPIKE

HEYWOOD

6.

5.

8   9.

7.

WALDEN   STREET

STREET

HUBBARD ST.

EVERETT ST.

LAUREL ST.

TREET

TON + MAINE RAILROAD

CONANTUM

TO WALDEN POND

◦ LEGEND ◦

1. MINUTE MAN STATUE
2. OLD MANSE
3. COLONIAL INN
4. MONUMENT SQUARE
5. 51 WALDEN / CONCORD PLAYERS
6. REUBEN HOUSE
7. EMERSON HOUSE
8. CONCORD MUSEUM
9. ORCHARD HOUSE AND SCHOOL
   OF PHILOSOPHY
10. THE WAYSIDE
11. GRAPEVINE COTTAGE
12. CONCORD FREE PUBLIC LIBRARY
13. THOREAU / ALCOTT HOUSE
14. NASHAWTUC HILL

Concord

STORIES TO BE TOLD

town memoirs (toun mem'wärs). 1. True stories that capture the spirit of a community, its genius loci. 2. Anecdotes passed on within a community from generation to generation. 3. A series of books by regional storytellers, illustrated by local artists, preserving the popular history of great American towns.

Concord

STORIES TO BE TOLD

A MASSACHUSETTS TOWN MEMOIR

BY LIZ NELSON • Illustrated by Amy Bishop

COMMONWEALTH EDITIONS

Beverly, Massachusetts

❖ DEDICATION ❖

To my husband, Philip, cherished always
In celebration of the history of Concord, where he grew up

Cover illustration: "A View of the Town of Concord," courtesy of the
Concord Museum, Concord, Massachusetts. www.concordmuseum.org.

Nelson, Liz, 1953–
    Concord: stories to be told / by Liz Nelson; illustrated by Amy Bishop
        p. cm -- (A Massachusetts town memoir)
    Includes bibliographical references.
    ISBN 1-889833-31-2
    1. Concord (Mass.)--History--Anecdotes. 2. Concord (Mass.)--
    Biography--Anecdotes.
    I. Bishop, Amy. II. Title. III. Town memoir.

Town Memoirs series editor: Liz Nelson
Cover and text designer: Jill Feron/Feron Design
Printed in the United States of America.

Commonwealth Editions is an imprint of Memoirs Unlimited, Inc.,
21 Lothrop Street, Beverly, Massachusetts 01915.

Visit our Web site at www.commonwealtheditions.com.

❖ CONTENTS ❖

NINETEENTH CENTURY

TWENTIETH CENTURY

❖ ACKNOWLEDGMENTS ❖

In writing this book, I am deeply indebted to Leslie Wilson, curator of Special Collections at Concord Free Public Library, for her expert guidance and remarkable ability to put her fingers on any material I sought. Beyond that, I thank the many Concordians going back generations who have so carefully kept records of Concord's history.

Many thanks to Leslie Wilson and Sarah Chapin for their careful review of my manuscript. I apologize for any errors that might remain; they are my responsibility.

A number of individuals in and outside of Concord kindly gave of their time and knowledge. I thank William Bailey, Robert Butman, Victoria Carr, Sarah Chapin, Robert Duncan, Marie Eaton, Mary and Mimi Emerson, Elizabeth Gardner, Phebe Ham, Bruce Irving (WGBH TV), Helen Kent, Margaret Kimball (Stanford University), John Manion, Anna Winter Rasmussen, Gordon Shaw, Annabelle Shepherd, Richard Smith, Judy Stern and Verna Tuttle (Concord Museum), Anita Tekle (Concord Town Clerk), Jan Turnquist (Orchard House), Teresa Wallace Ph.D (National Park Service), Joyce Woodman (Concord Free Public Library Special Collections), and the staff of the Massachusetts Archives.

As always, my family and friends shared my enthusiasm and offered support, helping me through the inevitable rough spots. Karen Marzloff's and Barbara Wilson's friendship and editorial feedback have been invaluable. Thank you all!

It has been a privilege and a pleasure to work with Amy Bishop as she chose scenes in the text and created her artistic gems. And finally, my thanks to publisher Webster Bull for the opportunity to write the book. I dedicate the story "Baseball Fans by the Thousands" to him.

—Liz Nelson, January 2002

1635   English settlers receive a grant to create "a plantation at Musketaquid . . . here after to be called Concord."

1639   First mill is built, a grist mill

1675–76 King Philip's War involves a number of Concordians

1687   First public school built

1729   Bedford incorporated, partially out of east Concord acreage

1735   Acton incorporated, largely of Concord land

1754   Lincoln incorporated, primarily as a result of religious differences

1775   Concord's population is approximately 1,500, about 265 families.

1775   **April 19** British Regulars march into town looking for supplies and exchange fire with Minute Men at the North Bridge

1780   Carlisle incorporated, taking land from northern area of Concord

1834   Ralph Waldo Emerson (1803–1882) moves to Concord

1843   Sam Staples jails Bronson Alcott (1799–1888) for nonpayment of taxes, which Alcott did as an act of protest. Three years later, Staples arrests and jails Henry David Thoreau for the same reason.

1844	Railroad comes to town
1845	Henry David Thoreau (1817–1862) begins his retreat at Walden Pond
1852	Nathaniel Hawthorne (1804–1864) buys Hillside from the Alcotts. Ephraim Bull introduces the Concord grape at the Massachusetts Horticultural Society
1868	Louisa May Alcott (1832–1888) writes *Little Women* at Orchard House, where her family had moved a decade earlier
1879	School of Philosophy opens for summer seminars
1886	Concord Antiquarian Society is formed, the present-day Concord Museum
1910	United States census lists Concord's population as 6,421 of whom 27 percent are foreign-born and another 20 percent second-generation immigrants
1938	Hurricane fells approximately 1,000 trees in town, but there's no loss of life
1951	Conantum, Concord's first major housing development, gets underway
1975	**April 18–19** Close to 40,000 protestors, celebrating the People's Bicentennial, camp on Minute Man National Park grounds
2000	Population of Concord is 15,537. Over 4,400 acres, almost 30 percent of land total, is protected in conservation.

SEVENTEENTH CENTURY

The Seventeenth Century

The place of grass and reeds—Musketaquid as the native people called it—became Concord in 1635. For the people who made their homes here, the century was marked by struggle. In the early decades, the Algonquian people struggled to survive an epidemic against which they had no resistance. The educated, idealistic group of English settlers who followed came with a form of government in mind and rigid Puritan tenets. However, farming in unfamiliar conditions severely challenged them. Initially they felt isolated by the distance from other settlements and vulnerable to attack because they were completely surrounded by land peopled by Native Americans. As more towns were founded west of Boston, Concord gradually grew into a regional trade center until, by the end of the 1600s, it became the "shire town," or county seat, where court sessions were held.

❖

THE PEOPLE OF MUSKETAQUID

On the periphery of the field, spring sun colored the oak trees green, and the air twittered with the calls of birds. A little distance away, the waters of the Musketaquid River flowed east. All appeared as it had always been. But the Algonquian woman knew better.

With practiced movements, she broke up the soil with her hoe made from a sea clam shell attached to a stick. Each time she planted, she placed a fish at her feet, then mixed ashes with the soil and built a small mound the width of two hands over the fish. With her thumb she poked corn kernels into the enriched earth, covered them, and patted the small hill with her palm. She worked all morning and then stopped, uncertain how many more mounds to create. How much did she and the other women even need to plant, when less than ten families remained in Musketaquid, "the place of grass and reeds"?

As the moon had waxed and waned, more native people had died. Through it all, the women stored their harvest and gathered nuts, berries, and roots. The men hunted and fished, and traveled along the river and the many well-worn woodland paths to other villages. In each, men and women spoke of little else except the numbers who had died and were dying still. In some villages they found the *weetus*, stick-framed dwellings covered in reed or bark mats, empty. They hadn't been dismantled, the frames left behind, the way native people left their wigwams as they moved with the seasons. These were villages where men, women, children old and young—all had died.

Permanent communities of native people had lived in New England for over 11,000 years. Historians know little more than the Algonquians did regarding exactly what plague decimated the native people in the early 1600s. Traders and fishermen, whom the native people called *Awaunaguss* (strangers), brought the disease with them from Europe. In the years 1616–1618, it killed between 75 and 90 percent of the Algonquian people who lived

How much did she and the other women need to plant, when less than ten families remained in Musketaquid, "the place of grass and reeds"?

along the New England coast and the inland villagers with whom they had contact. Then, within fifteen years of the plague, English settlers began to arrive in earnest.

THE TOWN GRANT

In 1630, John Winthrop, together with other English emigrants, sailed across the North Atlantic, royal charter in hand. The document provided that the new Massachusetts Bay Company, of which Winthrop was governor, would run its own affairs in a territory that stretched between what we know today as the Merrimack and Charles rivers. Seventeen ships brought over one thousand settlers that year—men and women seeking to build a new Puritan spiritual community and drawn by land and the opportunity it promised. Over the course of the next decade, twenty thousand more would follow.

Simon Willard arrived in 1634. Like many in the first migration, he was well-educated and of good social standing. Quickly he became involved in the lucrative fur trade, which sent him into the wilderness, away from the new villages sprinkled along the coast. Twenty-nine-year-old Willard wanted to establish a settlement inland, closer to the source of fur. At the Algonquian village of Musketaquid, with its few survivors, streams large and small flowed into two rivers, which in turn blended to form one. This offered abundant shad, salmon, and alewives, plus six potential mill sites. For decades the Algonquian villagers had cultivated the meadows and tracts of upland bordering the rivers, so the English immigrants would be spared the toil of clearing land for farming. Beyond stretched the forest, teeming with creatures whose fur Willard sought.

Though the Massachusetts Bay Company's General Court (the company's stockholders) likely found Willard's initiative impressive, they were not ready to have someone so young be a town founder. When the Reverend Peter Bulkeley arrived in Cambridge in 1635, Willard quickly befriended him. At fifty-two, Bulkeley was learned, respected, and quite wealthy; he brought with him £6,000. Willard, Bulkeley, and twelve families petitioned the authorities, and on September 2, 1635, the General Court issued the town grant:

> "It is ordered that there shall be a plantation att Musketaquid, and that there shall be 6 myles of land square to belonge to it . . . and the name of the place is changed and here after to be called Concord."

The new town was the first in New England settled above tide waters.

❖

SETTLING CONCORD

In the fall of 1635, a group of about sixty turned their backs on the relative security of Watertown and Cambridge and headed west into what they perceived as wilderness. Teams of oxen pulled carts carrying their few household goods and, most critically, six months of provisions to survive the winter, which would soon be upon them.

One account, sprinkled with hyperbole, written fifteen years later by Woburn resident Edward Johnson describes the travelers as making their way "through unknowne woods and through watery swamps." He wrote that "ragged bushes scratch their legs fouly . . . bloud trickle downe at every step . . . vere nere fainting [from the smell of sweet fern]" At night "watery clouds poure down . . . and sometimes the driving snow dissolving on their back."

Upon reaching Musketaquid, the men immediately set to work building shelters for themselves and their families. In the south side of the hill between what is now Monument Square and Merriam's Corner, the settlers dug into the hillside, drove posts into the ground, then created roofs out of bark and brush-wood covered with soil. In these primitive shelters, the Puritans endured the New England winter months.

Their Algonquian neighbors' food stocks helped them survive the first seasons. In the second year, settlers built single-gabled half houses for themselves. A large room downstairs had the entrance and chimney on the side and sometimes a loft above. All stood within a half mile of the meetinghouse, by order of the General Court, as protection against Indian attacks.

In 1637, Concordians officially purchased their land from the native people. Tradition tells that the transaction took place under Jethro's Tree (named after one of the Algonquians) near the southwest corner of the town square. Here, Simon Willard, and several others representing the Englishmen, met with five Algonquian people—Squaw Sachem ("Woman Chief"), Tahattawan, and Wibbacowet among them. The white men handed over payment: *wampum* (shell money), hatchets, hoes, knives, cotton cloth and shirts. Then Willard is said to have pointed north, south, east, and west and declared that he had bought three miles in each direction.

❖

EARLY STRUGGLES

Success in farming eluded Concord's early settlers. The meadows along the river flooded more than the Englishmen had anticipated, and they found the upland soil of poor quality, ill-suited for growing wheat and oats, and unresponsive to their efforts to fertilize it.

The families tried to nourish themselves with local fare—squash, corn, and pumpkins—but they missed familiar foods from their homeland. Grains such as wheat, barley, and rye, and basic fruit like apples and pears, were initially absent from their diets.

The town was so far removed from other plantations that loneliness enveloped many. In February 1639, Reverend Bulkeley wrote to his friend Thomas Shepard, "I am here shut up, and do neither see nor hear." Almost two years later, in a letter to John Cotton, he lamented, "I lose much in this retired wilderness in which I live."

The winter of 1641–42 was so severe that Governor Winthrop described "all the bay [in Boston as] frozen over . . . horses and carts went over in many places where ships have sailed." In Concord, families huddled in their homes, cattle died, and wolves attacked herds. People began to leave. Some returned to England, others to older communities, while a few ventured on to form new settlements.

But perhaps worst of all, the very accord among the people, which one tradition has as the source of the town's name, began to come apart. A second minister, the Reverend John Jones, had joined the settlement early on. Jones believed in the Covenant of Works, that the quality of an individual's life work determined his or her chance of salvation. Reverend Bulkeley, on the other hand, embraced the Covenant of Grace, a strict Calvinist view, whereby each person's fate was predestined. In 1644, Jones left Concord for Connecticut, taking his family and fifteen men, including two of Reverend Bulkeley's sons. Houses in Concord stood empty, with about fifty families remaining.

Townspeople petitioned the General Court, writing of "the povertie and meannesse of the place we live in not answering the labour bestowed on it" and asking that their "common charges," or colonial taxes, be reconsidered. Authorities responded by lowering the charges to £15 (in 1640 the town had paid £50), but they also issued an edict: "It is ordered that no man now inhabiting and settled in any of the s'd Townes (whether married or single) shall remove to any other Towne without the allowance of the majistrates or the select men of the towns." This prohibited families in three frontier towns—Concord, Sudbury, and Dedham—from leaving.

❖

THE TOWN COWS

Concordians, individually and as a community, kept the English tradition of taking care of indigent residents. When William Halsted died in 1645, he left £5 "unto the poore of the towne."

He specified that the money be used to purchase cows which would go to "such as are in need." One John Cotton had use of the "Towne Cowe" in the 1670s. In July 1698, Thomas Pellet, who took care of the meetinghouse and worked as the gravedigger, also benefited from Mr. Halsted's thoughtfulness. The selectmen ordered that the town cow (which, records noted, had a white face with black spots around each eye) be taken to him. There she was to remain until the selectmen judged Pellet's need to be less acute.

PIRATE TREASURE

The story passed from one generation to the next until Henry David Thoreau heard it and recorded it in his journal in 1854. One day, three pirates, believed to be members of Captain Kidd's crew, visited Ephraim Wood, one of Concord's early settlers. The pirates carried "a pair of old-fashioned deer-skin breeches, both legs full of coin," and they wished to bury the money in Wood's cellar. The farmer refused, but he did give them the earthen pots, shovels, and a lantern they demanded. The pirates slunk along the river bank and buried their treasure in a hollow. When they returned Wood's tools, the grateful villains also gave him a quart-sized hat filled with coins. Wood buried them in his cellar, but he was a poor man, and in time he retrieved the money and spent it. Treasure seekers have dug along the river, but the pirate's loot remains undiscovered to this day.

THE BROOKFIELD AMBUSH

The morning of August 2, 1675, dawned steaming with tension. At 8 A.M. Captain Edward Hutchinson and his company of twenty militiamen set out from Brookfield, an isolated settlement deep in Nipmuc country. Among them were Captain Thomas

Time and again, the Nipmuc shot burning arrows onto the roof.

Wheeler of Concord and his son. Their mission was to meet with leaders of the Nipmuc people and negotiate a peace agreement.

Two months earlier, hostilities had erupted between the native people of New England and white settlers in Plymouth Colony, signaling the beginning of King Philip's War. The "king" in question was Philip, sachem of the Wampanoag, who lived along the eastern shore of Narragansett Bay. He was known to his people as Metacom. Mistrust had been building for some time. In part this was a result of a complete lack of understanding of each other's culture, but also, undeniably, because of the Englishman's desire for more and more land. Massachusetts Bay Colony leaders desperately wanted to prevent Philip from drawing the Nipmuc, who lived across central Massachusetts, into the escalating war.

When Hutchinson and company arrived in the designated meeting place, about three miles from the village, not a single Native American showed himself. The men debated whether to proceed to the Nipmuc village or not. Cautiously, they ventured forth.

The trail grew narrow. On the right side rose a rocky hill, on the left lay a thick swamp. The men proceeded in single file for about one thousand feet. Shots rang out. In Captain Wheeler's words, about two hundred "perfidious Indians," hiding in the wetlands, opened fire. More lay hidden behind the Englishmen, cutting off their retreat. Several colonists lay dead on the ground. The rest clambered up the rocky incline.

Captain Wheeler stopped and turned to ascertain whether any of the fallen could be helped. The Nipmuc fired again. Wheeler's horse crumpled beneath him and the captain, also shot, fell to the ground. Further up the rise, his son scanned the rocky outcroppings and scraggly growth, searching for his father. Seeing no sign of him, he scrambled back down the hill. As he hoisted his wounded father onto a horse, musket shots exploded again, hitting young Wheeler in the arm. But he managed to run alongside his father until he caught a horse belonging to one of the dead, and finally they escaped beyond the range of Nipmuc guns. In the ambush, the native warriors killed eight men and wounded five, one of whom, Captain Hutchinson, would die of his injuries a few days later.

The survivors fled. They kept to open land as much as possible, constantly scouring the woods for signs of their pursuers. Wheeler later wrote that they did not even slow "to staunch the bleeding of our wounded men, for fear the enemy should have surprised us again." Despite having lost all three Brookfield men in the attack, they found their way back to the village, where they turned the largest house into a garrison. Sixty terrified villagers joined them. Two hours later the Nipmuc appeared, "sending in their shot amongst us like hail." They set fire to every structure in the settlement except the garrison. Then the siege began.

One young Englishman snuck out to fetch much-needed provisions. The natives killed him, decapitated him, and put his head on a pole for his compatriots to see. Just over a year later, at war's end, English colonists would likewise parade King Philip's head through the streets of Plymouth before they impaled it on a stake and left the flesh to rot.

Time and again, the Nipmuc shot burning arrows onto the roof. Settlers chopped holes in the shingles to beat out the flames. Then the Nipmuc set the side of the house on fire, but once again, the Englishmen put it out. On the third day, natives filled a cart with flax, hay, and other combustible materials. A sudden rainfall prevented the Nipmuc from lighting the contents and ramming the garrison with it, which likely saved the settlers' lives.

Twice, one of Hutchinson's men tried to slip out to get help. On his third attempt he succeeded, but rescue was already on its way. Travelers had seen smoke from the burning village and heard the exchange of gunfire. Seventy-year-old Major Simon Willard, one of the founders of Concord, arrived with forty-eight men on the third night. Finally, the Nipmuc withdrew.

Brookfield lay in ashes. Several weeks passed before Capt. Thomas Wheeler was strong enough to return to Concord, where he died fifteen months later. His son followed within a month. Approximately eight hundred settlers and three thousand Native Americans died in King Philip's War.

❖

JOHN HOAR'S STAND

John Hoar was "the only man in Concord who was willing to do it," wrote Major Daniel Gookin, Superintendent of the Indians. Willing, that is, during the winter of King Philip's War to offer haven to the Indians who had once called Musketaquid home.

Several hundred Native Americans had converted to Christianity in the decades after Puritans arrived in New England. In late August 1675, following the ambush in Brookfield, colonial authorities had ordered the Christian Indians confined to five "praying towns." One of these was Nashoba, part of present-day Littleton. But by November, even the restriction failed to ease settlers' fears, and authorities ordered the fifty-eight men, women, and children of Nashoba to Concord village.

Born in England and trained as a lawyer, John Hoar had come to the colony around 1640, and shortly thereafter had locked horns with colonial powers over several issues, including neglecting "the public worship of God on the Lord's day." In 1660, he moved to Concord. Eight years later, living up to his reputation as "rashly sharp of tongue and pen," Hoar described the Reverend Edward Bulkeley's blessing as "no better than vane babling," for which he was fined £10.

At the time of King Philip's War, he lived where the Orchard House now stands. (In fact, the Alcott home may contain parts of his house since Bronson Alcott put his dwelling together from two older houses that had stood on his land.) Here in wigwams, the unarmed Native Americans lived during the winter of 1675–76, "very soberly and quietly and industriously," according to Gookin. Beyond Concord, however, attacks on villages continued. In Framingham on February 1, the Nipmuc killed a settler's wife and three children. On February 10, warriors destroyed Lancaster's central village, killed several townspeople, and took twenty-four captive, including the minister's wife, Mary Rowlandson. Just a few days later, natives shot Isaac Shepherd, a farmer living on the outskirts of Concord, and kidnapped his young wife Mary.

A number of Concordians hated the presence of Native Americans among them and secretly sought the assistance of Captain Samuel Mosely. An exslaver and former privateer, Mosely played a key role in several battles of King Philip's War. His reputation for exceptional cruelty and indiscriminate hatred of Indians was widely known. He was happy to oblige.

On a Sunday in February 1676, Mosely arrived in Concord with his militiamen. At the meetinghouse, Mosely announced that "he understood there were some heathen in the town committed to one Hoar, which, he was informed, were a trouble and disquiet to them; therefore if they desired it, he would remove them to Boston."

Two or three Concordians voiced approval. Mosely took the silence of the rest as acquiescence. With his troops and about a hundred townspeople, he marched down the frost-hard road to John Hoar's house where he demanded to see the Indians. When Hoar assured him that they were secure, Mosely withdrew but left his corporal and several militiamen behind.

The next day, a pale sun did nothing to dispel the frigidity of the air. Samuel Mosely returned and insisted that Hoar give up the Indians. Hoar refused and the two men argued vehemently. Then Mosely ordered his corporal to remove all the Indians. One by one, the native people, all but a dozen of whom were women or children, filed past their protector. Mosely's men took them first to Charlestown and then shipped them out to Deer Island, to join hundreds of other Christian Indians.

John Hoar continued to follow the dictates of his conscience. Mary Rowlandson of Lancaster, taken captive in early February, had been sold to a Narragansett sachem, Quannopin. Colonial authorities sent Christian Indians, including Thomas Doublet, formerly of Nashoba, to negotiate her release several times. Finally, Quannopin agreed to a tentative ransom of £20 on the condition that John Hoar bring it. Hoar traveled unarmed deep into Algonquian territory and stayed for two days until a final agreement was reached. On May 2, 1676, at a place known thenceforth as Redemption Rock (in present-day Princeton, Massachusetts) Native Americans released Mary Rowlandson into the care of Englishman John Hoar and two Christian Indians.

At war's end in September 1676, colonial leaders ordered that all Indians involved in English deaths be killed and the remainder sold into slavery. Many of the Christian Indians on Deer Island had died from hunger and exposure. Some who survived lived out their lives as slaves in the colony; others were permitted to return to their villages. Major Gookin wrote that in November 1676, a number of Nashoba Indians returned to their plantation to live "quietly and unmolested." But as the seventeenth century gave way to the eighteenth, the native people of Musketaquid vanished from the vicinity as soundlessly as they had once paddled canoes down the river.

❖

SUNDAY DINNER

One Sunday in 1678, Thomas and Mary Pellit returned home from services at the meetinghouse to partake of the food that had been cooking over the fire during their absence. Their children contorted their faces in disgust as they ate, and almost immediately left the table and vomited. Mrs. Pellit checked the pot and found tobacco mixed in with her stew. She and her husband noticed three neighboring children laughing and "nickering." The Pellits pressed charges in court, and eight youngsters in all were fined for their "rudeness" and for "mischief done to the victuals of Thomas Pellit on the Lord's day."

TOWN BUSINESS

In 1638, Concord was fined five shillings by Massachusetts authorities for not having stocks in town to punish the errant, or a watch-house to keep an eye on hostile Indians. In 1660, the town faced a penalty of two shillings and six pence if they did not establish a "common house of entertainment" within twelve months. In the same year, town resident Richard Temple sued and collected twenty shillings in damages from John Gobble, who had called him a "lying rascal." In 1667, other weighty matters took up townspeople's time as they debated whether to repair the meetinghouse, where all town affairs were conducted, or build a new one.

Thirteen years later, citizens turned their attention to keeping the minister warm. They voted that any householder who owned a team of oxen should carry a load of wood to the minister's home each year. All others would be required one day a year to cut wood for their spiritual leader. The town also chose a committee to seat people at the meetinghouse—no small task since where one sat during services denoted one's status in town.

And shortly before the century ended, citizens voted to retire Reverend Edward Bulkeley since he was "under such infirmaties of body by reason of age." He was paid a pension of £30 a year.

EIGHTEENTH CENTURY

The Eighteenth Century

The 1700s began relatively quietly in Concord. The new colonial charter of 1691 was in place, and land grant questions had been resolved. Land, however, was becoming increasingly scarce, since it was subdivided among sons, generation after generation. Most farms were fifty acres or less, and the struggle for subsistence meant that children's education was often neglected. Concord had its least literate populace during the early decades of the eighteenth century: more men signed legal documents with a mark than at any other time in town history.

On the other hand, since Middlesex County court sessions were held here, an educated core of citizens resided in town, and by 1781, seven district schools were providing a rudimentary education. Over the course of fifty years, Bedford, Acton, Lincoln, and Carlisle incorporated on Concord's borders, in each case absorbing some of the town's acreage. Most significantly, Concord's pivotal role in the American Revolution earned it a lasting place in the nation's history that altered the town for all time.

THE TOWN POOR

Elizabeth Williams stood with her daughters, waiting for Concord's town meeting to adjourn. Three-year-old Mary leaned against her. Hannah had wrapped her little arms like a vine around her mother's neck, and occasionally Elizabeth supported her with one hand while she stroked her older daughter's shoulder with the other. For a few months she had tried to sustain her family, living off the provisions that remained after John left, supplemented by donations of milk, corn, and firewood from the town. Anxiously she waited, hoping her husband would come to his senses and return to his young family. John Williams never came back. By March 1734, his wife had no choice but to turn to the town for full support.

Ebenezer Meriam agreed to accept the lowest payment. He would provide room and board for the young mother and her two daughters for four months in return for ten shillings a week from the town. In addition, the town would pay for clothing and medical care when needed.

Year in, year out, mixed in with expenditures for highway work, keeping school, and bridge repair, the town treasurer reported payments for the subsistence of the town's poor. The vast majority were women, usually widowed, but some had been abandoned like Elizabeth Williams.

All communities in Massachusetts took care of the poor, but only their own. Most strangers who came into town were "warned out," asked to leave, not because they were vagrants, but because the townspeople wanted to be responsible only for those born in town or who married a resident.

Disputes arose between towns on a regular basis. Concord and Acton amicably resolved one in 1737 regarding widow Elisabeth Shepard. Concord agreed to pay two-thirds of her keep, Acton the balance. However, the case between Concord and Bedford over who was responsible for Daniel Roff and his wife ended up in

Elizabeth Williams stood with her daughters,
waiting for Concord's town meeting to adjourn.

court, with both communities incurring significant expenses. The court ruled in Concord's favor, and in February 1739 a constable was paid to move the Roffs to Bedford.

After Ebenezer Miriam, Lieutenant Hugh Brooks kept the Williams family for the next eight months. Then in February 1735, town records mentioned only one daughter, not two. At the end of the year, Hannah Williams, now four, was taken in by Joseph Wheat, and her mother's name disappeared from the pages. The last mention of a member of the Williams family was when the little girl was ten, and the town paid Dr. Prescott "for visiting and administering to Hannah Williams when she lay on her death bed." As was customary, other townspeople were compensated for providing her clothes for burial, a coffin, and digging her grave. The tavernkeeper was paid for "sundreys for the funeral."

❖

JOHN WHITING, REVEREND NO LONGER

John Whiting served as pastor of Concord's church for almost twenty years before his troubles began. On many a Sunday following the death of his wife in 1731, his head pounded viciously and his stomach roiled at the sight of food. In short, he had a hangover and was in no condition to preach. Town records note payments made to schoolmaster Timothy Minot for assisting Reverend White (appearing in his place) "on extraordinary occasions," but in time, townspeople asked whether these costs should be deducted from the reverend's salary. Ultimately, church members consulted with neighboring parishes, and finally, in 1738, Reverend Whiting resigned.

John Whiting may have stepped down from the pulpit, but he didn't exactly leave it. During his successor's sermons he sat where he had once stood and gazed out at his former parishioners. At the August 1739 town meeting, voters agreed "that the town will proceed to build a pew for Mr. John Whiting and his family . . . [and that] the selectmen [will] take care to build said pew as soon as conveniently they can at the towns cost." Three months later at the next town meeting, voters dismissed an article regarding "what the town will do about Mr. John Whiting's sitting in the pulpit." Presumably he now sat in his new pew.

Whiting died in 1752, and in the fall of 1774, at a town meeting otherwise devoted exclusively to pre-Revolutionary matters, townsmen voted "to dispose of the pew built for Mr. Whiting and his family in a public sale." The town moderator was promptly appointed the auctioneer, and the pew sold on the spot to the highest bidder for £18 13s 4d.

❖

BLISS'S UNBLISSFUL TENURE

Shortly after the Reverend Daniel Bliss took over as pastor in 1739, following John Whiting's resignation, the Concord church became so embroiled in controversy that parishioners surely must have yearned for the good old days when all they had to worry about was an intoxicated minister. A religious revival known as the Great Awakening was sweeping through New England, and Mr. Bliss turned out to be one of the most evangelical men of the cloth in the region. He preached in a bold, impassioned manner, creating considerable excitement amongst his audience. Church membership increased dramatically from the time of Bliss's ordination, when it stood at eighty-five. Fifty people joined in 1741, sixty-five in 1742. But his manner appalled the more traditional parishioners, and this created a schism in town that persisted until the Revolution.

Time and again, aggrieved church members convened councils to hear their complaints and issue rulings. Distraught parishioners felt the minister interpreted the Covenant of Grace far too loosely when he said that men could "go on in sins, in drunkenness, in Sabbath-breaking, even to rioting," because if you were among the chosen, "Christ will bring you home." These words the council judged to be a "very ill and unwarranted use of the doctrine of election." Alienated church members also accused Bliss of "wandering from town to town" to preach and "neglecting his own church at home." Yes, the council agreed, Reverend Bliss did travel a bit much, but there was no evidence he shirked his duties.

Sharp divisions continued. In 1744, churchgoers from the southeastern corner of town asked to be excused from paying the ministerial tax because they would be holding services separately. The town refused, so the forty-seven appellants turned to the General Court (the colonial legislative body), where they met with success. They formed a Second Parish and were exempted from paying the tax. In 1754, this parish became incorporated as the town of Lincoln.

Other distressed church members, including some of the most prominent men in town, organized the West Church in 1745. The town refused to let them worship in the meetinghouse, so they met for services at the Black Horse Tavern (which later would be the home of Nathan and Mary Brooks). Reverend Bliss's supporters called it the "black horse church." And discord in Concord went on and on and on.

❖

John Jack

Slave ownership twists through Concord's history as it does through that of most colonial communities. Among the slave owners were Benjamin and Elizabeth Barron. Benjamin likely saw the addition of two slaves to his household as proof of his success in land speculation, trade, and shoemaking. For his wife, though, slaves in her home must surely have revived buried memories. Elizabeth was none other than Betty Parris, daughter of the infamous Reverend Samuel Parris of Salem Village. It was nine-year-old Betty's and her cousin Abigail Williams's inexplicable fits, physical contortions, and gibberish that had instigated the Salem witchcraft hysteria of 1692. Betty and Abigail identified the Parrises' Native American slave, Tituba, as their tormenter. Soon thereafter, Betty's parents sent her away from home, and she had no further involvement in the accusations and travesties of justice that claimed twenty-five innocent lives.

Upon his death in 1754, Benjamin Barron's estate listed "One Negro servant named Jack [worth] £120" and "One Negro maid named Violet of no value," because apparently Violet was ill at the time. Betty inherited both slaves. And they, especially John Jack, as he was known, did not vanish from historic records unlike the slaves of Betty's childhood.

Years before the Massachusetts constitution abolished slavery, Jack was one of a number of slaves in New England who worked on the side to earn his liberty. Shortly after Betty Parris Barron's death, John Jack purchased his freedom from the Barron's daughter, Susanna. By 1761, he bought four acres of land from her, and in subsequent years he doubled his holdings. Besides farming, he supported himself by doing odd jobs around town and cobbling.

When John Jack died in 1773, he left a permanent reminder of his plight. His gravestone in the upper left corner of Old Hill Burying Ground bears an epitaph written by Daniel Bliss, son of the late minister. A Tory, Bliss saw the paradox in Patriots demanding rights for themselves while holding African American slaves. During the Revolutionary upheaval, a British officer sent the epitaph home, where it was published in a London newspaper. The words have been widely quoted and even translated into German, French, and Norwegian.

In 1830, members of the Middlesex Bar replaced what was by then a broken gravestone; however, the words etched into the gray slate remain unchanged.

God wills us free; man wills us slaves.
I will as God wills; God's will be done.
    Here lies the body of
    JOHN JACK
A native of Africa who died
March 1773, aged about 60 years.
Tho' born in a land of slavery,

He was born free.
Tho' he lived in a land of liberty,
He lived a slave.
Till by his honest, tho' stolen labors,
He acquired the source of slavery,
Which gave him his freedom;
Tho' not long before
Death, the grand tyrant,
Gave him his final emancipation,
And set him on a footing with kings.
Tho' a slave to vice,
He practised those virtues
Without which kings are but slaves.

❖

PRE-REVOLUTIONARY STEPS

In 1763, when the Seven Years' War in Europe ended, the British Parliament had a serious problem: a huge debt. To solve it and take care of planned expenses, they imposed taxes on the colonies. For generations, the English settlers in Massachusetts had had complete control over taxation. Local taxes had been voted on at annual town meetings, and provincial taxes had been determined by representatives elected to the General Court. No taxes had ever been paid to Britain, where colonists had absolutely no representation in Parliament.

In the mid 1760s, Parliament enacted a series of revenue-raising acts, only to repeal all but the tax on tea when colonists voiced their outrage. Concordians reacted cautiously. They reelected Charles Prescott as their representative though he was loyal to British policies. They also chose not to join in the boycotts of imported British luxuries in 1767, 1768, or 1770, though several Massachusetts towns did.

Beginning in 1767, however, a gradual shift began. Concord voters replaced Prescott with Captain James Barrett, who opposed the parliamentary measures. Nevertheless, when British troops arrived in Boston (to stifle the protests), Captain Barrett did not partake in talks of armed resistance; in fact, shortly hereafter, he accepted a contract to feed the Regulars oatmeal and other goods from his farm, an agreement he kept for six years.

In 1772, the British informed their colonial subjects that judges sitting on the colony's highest bench would in future be paid by Parliament rather than the General Court. Feeling that the jurists' impartiality might be compromised, nine of the most respected men in Concord gathered and wrote a document asserting their colonial rights. All but Daniel Bliss signed it.

In January 1774, three months after the Boston Tea Party, Concordians moved a step closer toward playing a central role in the nation's history. At a special town meeting, voters decided unanimously to boycott all British tea. Once again they put their sentiments in writing: "These Colonies have been and are Still illegally and unconstitutionally Taxed by the British Parliament as they are not Realy or Virtualy Represented therein."

The British, furious at the Boston radicals' act of dumping £10,000 worth of tea in the harbor, closed the port to all trade. Boston activists, in turn, initiated the Solemn League and Covenant; signers of this petition pledged neither to consume British products nor to do business with anyone who imported them. Concord townsmen met June 27, 1774, and endorsed the covenant, though they amended the original version slightly by drawing a line through the words that called for them to publish the names of nonconformists. The next day, town officials walked door to door, inviting adult males to sign. Massachusetts governor Thomas Gage had denounced the covenant and ordered the arrest of all who circulated it or added their names. Each individual who signed his name risked imprisonment. Nevertheless, by the end of the week, 280 Concordians (eight out of ten adult males in town) had signed. A handful of women did, too. Concord was one of seven towns in Massachusetts to endorse the covenant.

The British government moved to strengthen their control. They replaced the governor's council, previously chosen by the legislature, with Crown-appointed members and gave the governor the right to make all judicial appointments. Furthermore, they forbade towns from calling town meetings except for spring elections, violating a sacrosanct tradition that had served well for over a century (and continues to the present day). Townspeople were also no longer permitted to select their own juries.

Concord replied to what became known as the Coercive Acts by calling a county convention in August 1774. They resolved not to submit to the authority of any civil official appointed under the new system of government. Noting that two judges had accepted commissions since then, "we therefore look upon them utterly incapable of holding any office whatever." They also agreed that the next court session to be held in Concord would not be allowed to sit since the Coercive Acts violated the provincial charter of 1691. Finally, the group voted to hold a Massachusetts provincial meeting in Concord in early October. Their document closed,

> Our fathers left a fair inheritance to us . . . This we are resolved to transmit equally fair to our children after us . . . And if in support of our rights we are called to encounter even death, we are yet undaunted, sensible that he can never die too soon, who lays down his life in support of the laws and liberties of his country.

❖

CONFRONTATION AT THE COURTHOUSE

On September 13, 1774, ten justices arrived at Concord's courthouse to open the Court of General Sessions. But rather than presiding over the usual array of defendants, lawyers, and witnesses, the officials faced over one hundred men, many of them armed. Just two weeks earlier, county convention delegates had declared that as a consequence of Britain's Coercive Acts, courts should be suspended. The crowd was resolved not to let business be conducted as usual.

The justices took one look at the crowd, exchanged murmurs with each other, and judiciously chose to retreat.

They stood quietly shoulder to shoulder, barring the court-house door. The justices took one look at the crowd, exchanged murmurs with each other, and judiciously chose to retreat. Powdered wigs sitting squarely on their heads, their long robes billowing behind them, they walked to Ephraim Jones's tavern around the corner.

Shortly, a committee of five representatives of the people joined them. The justices proposed a compromise: they would open the court but conduct no business. The committee withdrew to consult with the crowd. Inside the tavern, the clock slowly ticked off the hours of the day. Finally, after the sun had set behind the courthouse, the committee returned with an answer—no. The justices saw no point in continuing and went home. No court sessions were held in Concord for the remainder of the year.

❖

THE MINUTE MEN

Governor Thomas Gage authorized town meetings throughout the province so that representatives could be elected to the next legislative session. In Concord, on September 26, 1774, townsmen did more than that. They agreed to raise, from the ranks of the militia, one or more companies of men who would "Stand at a minutes warning in Case of an alarm." Thus began the Minute Men.

Town meeting also approved the purchase of 7 1/2 barrels of powder, 56 pounds each, and 500 pounds of lead. It added a chest of firearms for the Minute Men. And voters chose a Committee of Correspondence to facilitate communication with other communities.

By late January 1775, 104 Concord men, most of them under twenty-five, formed the two Minute Men companies. Asserting once again that the dispute lay with Parliament, not with the Crown, they pledged "to the utmost of our power, [to] defend his Majesty, King George III, his person, crown and dignity. We will at the same time, to the utmost of our power and abilities, defend all and every one of our charter rights, liberties, and privileges; and will hold ourselves in readiness at a minute's warning with arms and ammunition this to do."

All in town knew who the Minute Men were; a stranger could identify one because he had his musket with him at all times, even at services in the meetinghouse.

❖

PROVINCIAL CONGRESS MEETS IN CONCORD

Governor Gage decided to move the 1774 session of the General Court to Salem, away from heated Boston emotions. Then he changed his mind and decided to cancel the session all together. However, the representatives convened on October 5 anyway. They resolved themselves into a Provincial Congress, thus becoming, for all intents and purposes, the elected governing body of Massachusetts. They also decided to continue their business October 11 at Concord's meetinghouse. Here, the congress elected John Hancock as its president and invited Concord's pastor, William Emerson, to officiate as chaplain. Soon after, their meetings adjourned to Cambridge, but the congress returned to Concord in March 1775, where they met frequently until war broke out.

❖

HIDE AND SEEK THE STORES

"This Month remarkable for the greatest
Events taking Place in the present Age."
—Reverend William Emerson in his journal, April 30, 1775

—〰—

Elnathan Jones, Joshua Bond, Willoughby Prescott, Jonas Heywood, and Colonel James Barrett stored 20,000 pounds of musket balls and cartridges, 206 tents, iron cannon balls, 51 wood axes, 24 boxes of candles, and 12 bushels of oatmeal. Thomas Jones hid 55 barrels of beef. A half dozen other Concordians took in 6 hogsheads of powder. Townspeople hid 7 loads of salt fish, 18 casks of wine, 20 casks of raisins, 50 barrels of salt, and 35,000 pounds of rice in fifteen different locations, including the town house.

In November 1774, the Provincial Congress had chosen to hide stores for use by the militia in Concord. The town lay along main routes to the west. Low hills surrounded the center, and the rivers created a natural barrier. That, together with the town's patriotic fervor, made Concord the perfect depot.

From Charlestown, Boston, Marblehead, and Salem, as well as other communities across Massachusetts, oxcarts rolled toward Concord village, packed with every conceivable supply a fighting force might need. Guards patrolled the North and South bridges, Bay Road, and the village green. The stores brought here at such risk must be protected, and should the Regulars appear, the alarm would be spread.

When the British troops appeared, though, no one was surprised. According to tradition, General Gage's wife, American-born Margaret Kemble Gage, shared British secrets with her compatriots. And, of course, men like Paul Revere kept a careful watch on troop movements.

On the other side, General Gage received constant communications from his own men who traveled through the towns and loyal Tories such as Concord's Daniel Bliss. Bliss's neighbors knew his sentiments well; he never hid them. They did not know, however, that one of their own, a member of the Provincial Congress, Dr. Benjamin Church, received handsome payment from the British for detailed reports on all that transpired in congressional meetings and in Concord itself. Dr. Church apparently needed extra funds to pay for a rather expensive mistress.

In mid-April, Paul Revere watched as men on British warships in Boston harbor lowered small boats off their decks and rowed them to shore. He rode to Lexington, where John Hancock and Samuel Adams were staying, to warn them that the British would likely strike soon. On April 17, provincial leaders ordered the

*At Joseph Hosmer's house, the Redcoats did not discover
the supply of ammunition because it was hidden under
the feather mattress upon which Hosmer's elderly mother lay.*

removal of most of the stores from Concord. Men used every available team of oxen and all through the night hauled arms and ammunition to neighboring Acton, Stow, and Harvard, as well as into the woods on Concord's periphery.

The following night, two lanterns beamed their message from the North Church steeple in Boston: the Regulars were coming by water. Paul Revere and William Dawes began their famous ride to warn fellow patriots. British sentries stopped them near the Lexington-Lincoln line, so neither made it to his destination. But Dr. Samuel Prescott of Concord had joined Revere and Dawes in Lexington. When the two messengers were stopped, Prescott spurred his mount, leaped over a stone wall, and galloped through the fields and country lanes he knew so well to warn the Concord Minute Men.

Approximately seven hundred Regulars marched into Concord in the early hours of April 19, weary and rattled by the unexpected confrontation in Lexington in which they had killed eight colonists; most, it was later determined, had been shot in the back. Carrying detailed lists and maps in hand (likely, courtesy of Benjamin Church), the British began to systematically search Concord homes.

They met with minimal success and even less cooperation. At Joseph Hosmer's house, for example, the Redcoats did not discover the supply of ammunition because it was hidden under the feather mattress upon which Hosmer's elderly mother lay.

General Gage's orders to Lieutenant Colonel Smith, commander of the expedition to Concord stated, "You will take care that the soldiers do not plunder the inhabitants, or hurt private property." As a result, British officers generally behaved with restraint. At Amos Wood's house, when they were led to believe that ladies were hiding behind a locked door, they didn't break it down. Militia supplies were behind the door, not ladies.

Timothy Wheeler, in whose mill barrels of flour were stored, is reported to have held a handful of his own flour over a barrel and said, "This is *my* flour." Soldiers responded by saying they were not there to seize private property. Elsewhere, though, they broke open dozens of flour barrels and rolled some into the millpond. Patriots retrieved them a few days later and fished out and saved the iron cannon balls and lead musket balls, which they had hidden in the flour.

At Ephraim Jones's tavern, servant Hannah Barnes pleaded with the Regulars. The room they wanted to search, said she, was her own private room. The soldiers politely let her be and never saw the chestful of provincial money on the other side of the door.

Not all were so gallant or honest. Troops stole saddles and bridles from a stable, a two-volume Bible from the meetinghouse, and an assortment of household goods from another private home. In the center of town, they burnt carriage wheels, some barrels, and the liberty pole. Sparks ignited the courthouse roof, and the sight of smoke alarmed the militia gathered above the river, precipitating the confrontation at the North Bridge. For the most part, however, the Redcoats retreated from Concord empty-handed, which was the least of their problems that day.

❖

HARVARD COLLEGE AT CONCORD

Not long after the skirmish between the Minute Men and British Regulars at North Bridge and the ignominious retreat by the Redcoats, the Reverend William Emerson rode to Cambridge to get a firsthand look at the state of affairs. Provincial troops milled around the town common and Harvard Yard, awaiting further orders. Some of the college buildings had been converted to barracks. Concord's pastor suggested his hometown would serve well as a temporary campus for Harvard College, and after due consideration, the administration gratefully accepted. On June 17, 1775, the Harvard College library moved to Concord while patriots fought at Bunker Hill. In October, the 1775–76 academic year got underway. The faculty and 143 students boarded in Concord homes and walked to their classes held at the town house and meetinghouse. Once the British Regulars withdrew from Boston in March 1776, Harvard resumed classes in Cambridge. In June, President Samuel Langdon sent a letter to Concord gratefully acknowledging "the many tokens of your friendship . . . and the use of your public buildings." He also expressed the hope that the students had behaved themselves and "that you will readily forgive any errors which may be attributed to the inadvertence of youth."

❖

A FAMILY DIVIDED

In the afternoon of March 20, 1775, Captain Brown and Ensign De Berniere of the British army had moved briskly through Concord. They surveyed the town surreptitiously and then stopped to ask directions to the home of Daniel Bliss. Upon reaching it, they were warmly received, and Bliss readily answered their many questions regarding the political tenor of the town, the number of cannon present, stores of food, and the presence of guards.

One of the Englishmen predicted to his host that, despite their preparations, Americans would not fight. Bliss shook his head and gestured to his brother Thomas Theodore, who happened to be passing, "There goes a man who will fight you in blood up to his knees!"

The Blisses were a family divided. It would appear that the Reverend Mr. Bliss's sons absorbed their father's fervor but applied it to politics rather than religion. Two sons stood tall as supporters of the British monarch and government, while two were ardent patriots. Their sister, Phebe, was married to the Reverend William Emerson, a man also sharply opposed to the actions of parliament. On many occasions, lawyer Daniel Bliss, eloquent and Harvard-educated, publicly expressed his views: Provincials were foolish to think they could oppose so powerful a nation as Britain. He was also quick to note what he saw as the patriots' hypocrisy. How could they decry parliament's virtual enslavement of the colonies when their leaders—Colonel James Barrett and Reverend William Emerson among them—were themselves slave owners?

Captain Brown and Ensign De Berniere stayed for dinner that March evening. According to the latter's account, while they continued to discuss the mounting political tension, Bliss received word that having noted he was entertaining British spies, townspeople "should not let him go out of town alive that morning." The British invited Bliss to leave with them. Once night, with all its protective shades of black, settled in, Daniel Bliss bade farewell to his wife and children and left his native town. He would never return.

A few weeks later, Samuel Bliss, also a Tory, came to Concord to make arrangements for his brother's family to depart for the safety of British-controlled Boston. Concordians subsequently arrested him on suspicion of having provided Regulars with information. On May 12 they brought him before Duncan Ingraham for a hearing. However, four witnesses testified that Samuel Bliss had been in Boston all day on April 19. Ingraham released Bliss, who promptly fled to Boston as well.

Samuel, like his brother Daniel, joined the British army. Before the war ended, he attained the rank of captain. He then retired from the army and settled among the many Tory refugees in New Brunswick. Colonel Daniel Bliss was stationed in Quebec during the fighting. When hostilities ended, he also moved to New Brunswick, where he once again took up the practice of law. The same qualities that had contributed to his prominent social standing in Concord—integrity, clear and logical thinking, fine wit— helped him to rise quickly in his new home, too. Within a few years, Daniel Bliss became Chief Justice of the Court of Common Pleas.

Thomas Theodore Bliss joined the patriot army as a captain. His fighting days were cut short, though. During Benedict Arnold's expedition against Quebec in the winter of 1775–76, the British took him captive and for the next several years moved him from one prison to the next. Story has it that when Daniel Bliss heard his younger brother was a prisoner of war, he used his considerable influence with General Gage to prevent Thomas from being freed early or exchanged.

Joseph Bliss, at eighteen the youngest of the four, was working as a clerk in Henry Knox's bookstore in Boston when war broke out. He also joined the Continental Army, serving in his employer's artillery regiment. Against all odds, Knox's men managed to move captured cannon from Fort Ticonderoga, through what is now New York state, across the Berkshire Mountains, and finally to Boston, where their presence finally forced the British army to evacuate.

To the best of anyone's knowledge, Daniel Bliss never again communicated with his family in Massachusetts. Massachusetts, however, had not finished with him. In November 1780, he was tried *in absentia* and found guilty of "levying war and conspiring to levy war against the Government and People of this Province, Colony, and State." His estate was the only one in Concord confiscated by the General Court, and in March 1781, the government sold it at auction for £278.

❖

John Cuming, Physician Plus

In 1746, John Cuming left Harvard College a year before graduating to continue his education and get medical training in Britain. If the college felt slighted, it recovered, because twenty-five years later it awarded Dr. Cuming an honorary masters degree, noting his fame as physician and surgeon. Military officer, town moderator, justice of the peace, president of the Court of General Sessions, land speculator, member of Concord's Committee of Correspondence, Inspection and Safety, member of the House of Representatives, and delegate to the Massachusetts constitutional convention—for John Cuming all these titles could be added to that of physician.

Upon returning from his medical studies abroad, John Cuming fought as a British officer in King George's War on the New England frontier. Back in Concord in 1753, he married Abigail Wesson, and the couple had one daughter, born in 1755. In the same year, Cuming headed north again to fight in the French and Indian War as a lieutenant colonel. He was shot and captured, and the musket ball that lodged in his hip remained there for the rest of his life. Eventually a Frenchman arranged a prisoner exchange.

Home once more, he established a medical practice respected throughout Middlesex County. His epitaph captures his reputation: "his hand was as charitable as healing to the poor." Story has it that he never charged a patient he treated on the Sabbath.

In the early 1760s, Dr. Cuming added to the two hundred acres he owned in Concord with purchases of land in New Hampshire, Vermont, and western Massachusetts. Cummington, Massachusetts, is named for him. At the same time, he began serving as moderator of Concord's town meetings. Townsmen chose him ninety times between 1763 and 1788 to keep their gatherings orderly. With one noteworthy interruption.

In 1774, when 80 percent of Concord's townspeople signed the Solemn League and Covenant, pledging not to consume British goods, John Cuming was not among them. As Crown-appointed justice of the peace, he had sworn to "uphold the king's law," and pre-Revolutionary activities likely thrust him into wrenching inner dialogues. Patriots took note of the absence of his signature, and over the next nine months, citizens at town meeting chose him to moderate only one of eight meetings.

Always the physician at heart, after the confrontation at the North Bridge on April 19, 1775, John Cuming treated wounded British soldiers (at Daniel Bliss's home, fittingly). By early 1776, Cuming must have made his position clear, and no one doubted his patriotism. He was chosen for the Committee of Correspondence, Inspection, and Safety, where he served, with a short break, until the end of the war. Just before the signing of the Declaration of Independence, the Provincial army sought experienced officers from prior wars, and the General Court appointed him brigadeer general and ordered him to lead three thousand troops to Fort Ticonderoga.

However, once again, John Cuming wrestled with a decision. Maybe the tales of captivity he had told his wife had been too vivid, for she adamantly opposed his heading north to fight. His friend Reverend Emerson found the doctor "very low in Spirits and exceedingly cast down." Mrs. Cuming prevailed, and her husband resigned his commission, devoting his energy to fighting the war from home, instead. Besides his work on the Committee of Correspondence, he served as representative to the General Court, and in 1779, townsmen chose him as their delegate to the state constitutional convention, which met in Cambridge to write the constitution of the Commonwealth of Massachusetts.

John Cuming died in 1788 at age sixty and lies buried at the Old Hill Burying Ground. Among the bequests from his sizable estate, he left £300 sterling, half to benefit private schools in Concord, half to be distributed among the poor. To two of his former slaves, he left £35 each. And, first and foremost a physician, he gave £300 to Harvard College, the income of which was to be used for a professorship of medicine. The college combined his bequest with other funds to create Harvard Medical School.

❖

1792 SMALLPOX EPIDEMIC

At the corner of Fairhaven Road and Route 2, lies Concord's smallest public burial ground, measuring a mere twenty-five by thirty-five feet. In the middle of this untended woodsy plot, surrounded by remnants of stone walls, two stones mark the grave of Sarah Potter, a victim of the smallpox epidemic of 1792. It is believed that the other nine victims lie buried here, as well. It was considered improper to bury them in regular cemeteries.

Sarah Potter, age sixty, died first. Benjamin Hosmer lost his young wife and infant to the disease, too. The Potter home became the "pest house" or innoculation hospital, and 130 townspeople came for the vaccine the year of the epidemic. The new medical procedure was controversial for good reason: Two of the ten who died in Concord did so as a result of the innoculation. Sarah Potter's grave marker notes that she "died of the small pox taken in the natural way."

❖

BEES, BARTERING AND CASH

Harvested corn lay in piles like haystacks in the farmer's barn. Neighbors and friends of all ages, but especially men and boys, milled around, grabbing at ears of corn and deftly removing the husks. Within easy reach stood a mug of toddy rum (diluted and sweetened rum), for no gathering was complete without an ample supply of drink. Once the husking was over, the farmer served pies, crackers, and cheese, and, satisfied, one and all returned home.

Bees of all kinds took place on a regular basis in small towns such as Concord through the early nineteenth century. At apple bees, women gathered to prepare the fruit for drying or for making huge quantities of applesauce, which had to last until the next harvest. They also met in quilting bees, still common today.

Such gatherings were an expression of community living, but they were also a result of a limited supply of currency. People bartered for goods and services and lived on credit. Most farmers had accounts in local stores, and they paid their creditors with proceeds from selling surplus produce or with the produce itself.

During the Revolutionary War and in the years that followed, the cash in circulation was terribly unstable. Every town's resources were stretched thin. Few farmers had surplus produce for barter. Inflation raged, and all of Massachusetts sank into a deep depression. Many in Concord, and elsewhere, were in danger of losing their land or landing in debtors' prison.

Captain Daniel Smith lived in Concord and ran a store on the spot where the town hall now stands. Like a number of others in town, he improved his cash flow quite simply—by printing and passing counterfeit bills. Forgery was widespread in the country. Until Jacob Perkins of Newbuyport invented his intricate, steel-plate printing method in the early 1800s, banks' use of copper plates made counterfeiting relatively easy. Captain Smith's fortune took a turn he had not bargained for, though. He was arrested, convicted, and sent to state prison.

NINETEENTH CENTURY

The Nineteenth Century

Change marked this century in Concord. Ralph Waldo Emerson's move to the town of his ancestors permanently affected the intellectual tenor. Not only did he mentor local genius Henry David Thoreau, but he also drew to Concord intellectuals and reformers such as Margaret Fuller, Frank Sanborn, Bronson Alcott, Ellery Channing, and Elizabeth Peabody. The writers residing here in the 1800s became known as the Concord Authors. The coming of the railroad in 1844 opened new markets and changed agricultural practices. Farmers switched to profitable dairy farms, increased their fruit production and became famous for their crops of strawberries and asparagus. The railroad also brought the first immigrants to Concord—the Irish who laid the tracks. They would be followed in the last decades of the century by Nova Scotians, Norwegians, and Italians, leavening Concord's Yankee population.

VOTING LINES

Two lines snaked along opposite sides of town square. Though voting at the poll would be private, men had no compunction whatever about showing which candidate they supported by joining the appropriate queue outside. In 1802, voters kept a close watch on the numbers in line, and when they realized the election was tied, one side sent a group to pull a sick neighbor from his bed. They carried him to the booth, where he broke the deadlock; Concord voted for candidate Strong for governor, 92 to 91. Statewide, Strong enjoyed a majority vote, too.

❖

COURT DAYS

Dozens of wagons, carriages, and chaises stood in front of the Middlesex Hotel on Monument Square and lined the streets nearby. Horses took up every space in village barns and sheds, and their owners filled the three taverns in town. On occasion, plaintiffs, jurors, lawyers, and judges boarded at local homes, as well. Every year, during the second week of September, Concord vibrated with energy. Court was in session.

Each morning the court bell summoned the participants. The uniformed sheriff, wearing a sword at his hip, and deputies, holding their staves, waited for the judge at the tavern door and escorted him to the courthouse. Inside, besides the usual characters associated with legal cases, dozens of citizens filled spectator seats. For many, court days relieved the grind of farm life and were not to be missed. In a good year, the audience might be treated to a captivating murder case or the oratory of Daniel Webster or esteemed resident Samuel Hoar. And if the drama within failed to meet expectations, entertainment abounded outside.

They dragged the offending woman out of the house
and placed her astride a rail.

A row of booths and stands ran the length of the common in front of the meetinghouse. Merchants sold rum, gin, brandy, wine, beer, flip (spiced ale or cider, served hot), and toddy. Other carts offered baked goods, candies, and fruit aplenty. Peddlers flourished their wares, and even horse traders came, hoping to strike a good deal. Several large booths were set up for dancing, with fiddlers strolling nearby ready to burst into tune. Many from around Middlesex County came just for the fairlike atmosphere in the square; children were not really expected to attend school.

Long after the judge had pounded his gavel to adjourn court for the day, revelers continued to drink, dance, and make merry, all the while taking care, one would hope, not to find themselves in the defendant's seat at a subsequent court session.

❖

She Rode Out on a Rail

The young men gathered, their tongues wagging. During September court days, Concord always buzzed with activity, but they could not countenance the introduction of this new element in town. Word had spread that one Huldah Williams, herself of low repute, had invited a harlot to her two-room house on Lexington Road, presumably to entertain those inclined to wanton pleasures. As Edward Jarvis told the tale, the men resolved "to remove this foul blot offered to the character of Concord." One evening, they marched to the small house, prepared to remove the harlot should she not agree to leave voluntarily. She did not. They dragged the offending woman out of the house and placed her astride a rail, which they had brought along for just such an exigency. Two or three men shouldered each end of the rail, a man walked on each side of her to prevent her from toppling off, and the rest spread themselves around the makeshift means of transportation. Upon reaching the town line, they derailed the woman, warning her never to step foot in Concord again.

"Everyone rejoiced and honored the deed," wrote Jarvis. Though some worried that legal authorities might look askance at such vigilante behavior, no action against the young men was ever taken.

CONCORD FEMALE CHARITABLE SOCIETY

> Feeling it to be the duty of everyone, as far as is in his power, to relieve the wants of the indigent and distressed, and thinking that more good can be done by united efforts than by individual charity, we, the subscribers, in order to perform this duty in the best manner, do agree to form ourselves into an association.

Thus, the Concord Female Charitable Society, the first organized women's group in town, was born in 1814. Open membership drew over seventy women, who elected an executive board, and the society immediately transformed words into deeds. Used clothing was collected and kept in a sack, and members' dollar-per-year dues paid for purchases of provisions, fabrics, and yarn. The women bought a bushel each of rye and corn, ready to be donated as needed. Six yards of gingham went directly to widow Hannah Hunt, a flannel waistcoat to Mrs. Holden, and a woolen frock from the sack to Sally Brown. Sheets, pillow cases, straw bonnets, and shoes found new owners. In the first six months, the women gave out eighty-nine garments. And meat was purchased for Mrs. Greenough.

While meticulous records from the early decades note donations of flour, rice, raisins, and molasses, the most frequently distributed items were tea and sugar. Prior to the days of temperance, the women, on occasion, gave wine, brandy and gin to offset hard times as well.

In 1826, *The Concord Freeman* praised the women's efforts saying "it is evident they [charitable societies] do much good in various ways." But a number of men in town dismissed the women's work and referred to them as the "chattable society."

The women continued to meet every fortnight, to collect, sew, and distribute, and yes, probably chat. In the long history of the society, the membership has included the mothers, daughters, and wives of most of the prominent men in town. Squire Samuel Hoar's wife and daughter were members, as was Thoreau's mother, who joined in 1825 and belonged for the rest of her life. Ralph Waldo Emerson's mother, wife, and daughter all were members at one time. Mary Merrick Brooks, Mrs. Francis Jarvis, and Mrs. Lemuel Shattuck all contributed their efforts to the society as well.

In the 1860s, however, interest began to wane, and in 1867, the women met to consider disbanding. Instead, they addressed criticisms and resolved disagreements. Not only did they continue their work in Concord, in years to come they sent help beyond town limits—to victims of fires and other disasters. In addition, the women assisted when other local societies were created. In 1886, when the Home for the Aged opened in town, the Concord Female Charitable Society made sheets and pillowcases.

The nineteenth century gave way to the twentieth. Concord's women went on meeting every two weeks. Over time, bequests from former members and the purchase of securities added to the society's operating budget. During the Great Depression, attendance at sewing meetings rose to over twenty. The women made clothing for infants and children and mended items for the hospital. They distributed thousands of quarts of milk and paid for hospital visits, dental care, and medicine. They scoured rummage sales, picking up dozens of pairs of shoes to pass along. As soon as the cold weather set in, their president wrote, requests for clothing, blankets, and footwear poured in daily, sometimes four or five a day.

In 1942, the Concord Female Charitable Society renamed itself the Concord Friendly Aid Society. Their work remained the same, though they now sent children to summer camps, too. By 1950, the society hired a social worker who directed distribution of aid. However, as the state assumed responsibility for social welfare, the women's mission began to shift. In 1956, the name changed once more to the Concord Family Service Society, and its chief purpose became to strengthen family relationships in times of crisis. That year, over three hundred people took advantage of the services provided, seeking support through marital problems, unemployment, physical and mental illness, and single parenthood.

Today, the Concord Family Service Society serves individuals not only in Concord, but also in eleven area towns. Its funding comes from investment income, state and federal monies, Community Chests, and the United Way, as well as hundreds of individual donors, known as Family Friends, and over two dozen corporations and businesses. The society offers individual, couple, family, and group counseling, foster care, pregnancy counseling, employee assistance programs, and referrals. Its fundamental goal remains unchanged: to relieve the distressed by united effort.

❖

WANTON SLAUGHTER

Much to the boys' delight, the last Wednesday in May dawned clear and dry. In Boston, the governor would be inaugurated that day, but at Nine Acre Corner where Concord's youth gathered, birds were on their minds, not politics.

As they did every Election Day (as it was known), Edward Jarvis, his brothers, and dozens of boys, milled around, guns resting on their shoulders, pouches hanging at their sides. Some jostled each other; others strutted, while the younger ones shifted from foot to foot on the periphery. Two "captains" silenced the group and, taking turns, began to call out names, choosing sides. Edward, young, slight, and a hopelessly poor shot, was among the last picked.

With allegiances established, the boys dispersed, each headed to his favorite patch of woods or meadow in search of anything with feathers. The goal for the day was to shoot as many birds as possible, though crows and hawks were the most prized, and to raid as many nests as they could.

Late in the afternoon, the boys gathered again. Each side laid out the dead birds in piles, assigned each carcass its value, and then determined who the individual winner was and which side had won.

Then, one at a time, they placed the stolen eggs on a smooth spot. Any fearless hunter who wished could approach the egg blindfolded and flail at it with a stick. If he broke the egg, all cheered. If he missed, someone took his place. "Happily," wrote Jarvis, "this single day's indulgence in cruelty" ended in the early 1820s.

❖

The Concord Lyceum

"The one hundred and twenty-five dollars which is subscribed in this town every winter for a Lyceum is better spent than any other equal sum."
—Henry David Thoreau in his journal, 1852

Beginning in 1829, Concord's men, women, and young people had access to an extraordinary array of lectures at its newly founded lyceum. They listened to speakers expound on the history of Rome, the Jesuits, or the Siege of Quebec, on the lives of Martin Luther, Plato, or Benjamin Franklin. Experts presented information on honey bees, caves, and water. Educational issues, philosophy, religion, travel (from Cuba to Lake Superior to Palestine), and current events (such as capital punishment, rights of women, and temperance) all found a place among the 784 lectures featured in Concord during the lyceum's first fifty years.

Concord's lyceum was one of seventy-eight created in the state between 1826 and 1830. Though not the first (that honor goes to the lyceum in Millbury, Massachusetts), it was among the longest lasting. In January 1829, the Reverend Bernard Whitman gave the first lecture, on "Popular Superstitions." Three hundred people attended, and the immensely popular events were off and running.

The lectures played a social role, too, as Ebenezer Hoar noted in his speech at the lyceum's fiftieth anniversary: "The young men and maidens [attend] sometimes, perhaps with other views than strictly intellectual culture." Adults encouraged school boys to attend, mindful of the lyceum's purpose—"improvement in knowledge, the advancement of Popular Education, and the diffusion of useful information throughout the community." At times, however, the youths' presence was a source of embarrassment and annoyance since they were less tolerant of the occasional mind-numbing speaker. In 1845, the board chose five adults to keep order.

In its first decade, debates were also included in the program, in part because the Concord Debating Club had merged with the lyceum in 1829. Questions such as "Ought imprisonment for debtors be abolished?" "Ought corporal punishment be used in schools?" "Ought the reading of novels be encouraged?" and "Should literary and scientific degrees be conferred upon women?" drew large crowds and often lasted for several evenings.

Ralph Waldo Emerson addressed his fellow citizens one hundred times, Thoreau nineteen. Dr. Edward Jarvis gave seventeen lectures, Frank B. Sanborn seven. Samuel Hoar, Bronson Alcott, historian Lemuel Shattuck, poet William Channing, and horticulturist Ephraim Bull all contributed. And with men like Emerson as magnets, Concord attracted the best speakers in the country. Oliver Wendell Holmes, Theodore Parker, Horace Greeley, Louis Agassiz, James Russell Lowell, Horace Mann, Charles Sumner, Henry Ward Beecher, Henry James, and Wendell Phillips all spoke.

In the 1840s, interest in debates waned and after the Civil War so did the public's interest in serious topics. The calendar of events leaned more toward entertainment, comedy, and music rather than lectures. Nevertheless, at its fiftieth anniversary in 1879, the lyceum still played a significant role in Concord's social and intellectual life. World War I eventually brought about its demise. In their final report of March 1921, the directors wrote, "All signs seem to indicate that the purpose for which [the lyceum] was organized and the conditions under which it has lived for so many years, no longer exist."

❖

CONCORD'S BICENTENNIAL

"For the most part, the town has deserved the name it wears.
I find our annals marked with a uniform good sense.
I find no ridiculous laws, no eaves-dropping legislators,
no hanging of witches, no ghosts, no whipping of quakers,
no unnatural crimes."
—Ralph Waldo Emerson in his bicentennial address

At town meeting in April 1835, voters overwhelmingly approved an article calling for Concord to celebrate its bicentennial September 12, 1835. Concord's date of incorporation was September 2. But they were right to adjust the date.

One hundred and seventy years after their European neighbors adopted the Gregorian calendar (which we use today), Great Britain and her colonies finally decided to do the same. In order to restore the vernal equinox to March 21, by the middle of the 1700s eleven days had to be dropped from the calendar. Citizens on both sides of the Atlantic went to bed September 2, 1752, and woke up the next morning eleven days further on.

Agreeing on a corrected date proved to be one of the few points on which all concurred. Many wanted the observance to be a local affair, involving all citizens with ties to Concord, rather like a homecoming. They argued for a simple, inexpensive meal, local speakers, some singing, and a service in the meetinghouse. Others envisioned a far grander celebration. They wanted to invite notable speakers from afar and to serve a magnificent meal.

The well-heeled faction prevailed. They invited first Daniel Webster, then the illustrious Edward Everett, as orators. Both declined. Finally, after much hand-wringing, they approached Ralph Waldo Emerson, who graciously accepted.

The committee opted for an elaborate meal that many Concordians simply could not afford. Discontent erupted in a furious letter to the *Concord Freeman*, signed by A Native-Born Citizen of Concord. The writer claimed "ARISTOCRATS [his capitals] were going to have another frolic at the expense of Farmers and Mechanics [manual laborers], whom they despise." Boycott the bicentennial, he urged readers! Despite the rancor, Concord celebrated. Once the order of the procession had been settled (should the artillery or the infantry lead?), it moved smoothly down Concord's major roads past schoolchildren flanking the route. Four hundred people, including the governor, judges, and members of Congress, dined on delectable fare. Many of the guests spoke, too, but only young Waldo Emerson captured the hearts of Concordians.

While men dined under the tent and listened to the speakers, the ladies gathered in the courthouse for a collation, supplied by the women themselves and free to anyone who had managed to get a ticket. Though many stayed away from this event as well, a letter to the editor a week later, from "The wife of a Middlesex Farmer," insisted there had been a "reciprocity of entire good feeling between the citizens generally" and that ladies of leisure mixed with those in "humbler walks of life without any inequality or distinction."

As if the planning of the event had not been challenging enough, once it was all over, the committee found it had overspent its town-allotted budget by a hefty $100. However, the event that started with agreement as to the date, ended with agreement regarding finances. Under no circumstances did committee members want to ask townsmen for more money and risk hearing more complaints. They divided the overrun equally among themselves and paid the remaining bills out of their own pockets.

❖

JOSIAH BARTLETT:
A PHYSICIAN FOR OVER HALF A CENTURY

Thank heaven, there are some things money will not buy. It cannot buy position. It cannot buy confidence of the community; it cannot buy the love and affection of the hundreds to whom we have ministered in the hour of danger, sorrow, and suffering. Above all, it cannot buy the consciousness that we have done our duty in this conflict of life, when it is almost ended. It pays him well who does his duty well.
—Dr. Josiah Bartlett, on the art of practicing medicine

—⚬—

Snow lay deep across the land in dazzling white splendor, and Dr. Josiah Bartlett wasn't going anywhere. Not that he didn't try. First he ventured out in his sleigh. After it overturned several times, he switched to his horse, but the poor creature floundered in a chest-high drift. Dr. Bartlett slid out of the saddle, down the horse's hindquarters, and man and beast found themselves struggling in the snow. Finally, he gave up and returned home. Regardless of foul weather, his own ill health, or a patient's inability to pay, Dr. Bartlett always went when called. This was the only time in fifty years that he failed to reach a patient in need.

An avid reader, Dr. Bartlett was also a subscriber to the Concord Lyceum. He was a member of the Social Circle, a private men's club, for fifty years. And he was an active abolitionist, on many occasions driving fugitives to the next safe house on their journey to freedom. But he devoted still more of his energy to the temperance movement.

After a decade of practicing medicine, Bartlett was convinced that alcohol reduces a person's ability to resist disease or recover from injury. In 1832, he joined the local temperance society and began talking with tavernkeepers and merchants, trying in vain to persuade them not to serve liquor. His passionate views were well-known, and since he lived on Lowell Road, a mere one hundred yards from a tavern, he was the target of vandalism several times. Drunks girdled all his apple trees one night, cutting away bands of bark and thus destroying them. Another time, they threw a bottle of acid into his home, shattering a window and destroying the carpet where it landed. One morning, the doctor woke to find men had shredded the top of his chaise and cut off his horse's tail. Bartlett drove his vehicle around town just as the vandals had left it, to further make his point about the effects of alcohol.

At a temperance meeting, when someone pointed out that it was easy for him to oppose drinking, in which he didn't indulge, while he persisted in "the filthy habit of chewing [tobacco] which was as bad, or worse," Bartlett threw his wad in the fire and never touched tobacco again.

Years later, Dr. Bartlett would be the victim of a drunk driver who careened his wagon into the doctor's chaise, overturning it and breaking the doctor's leg. Josiah Bartlett limped for the rest of his life, and in his senior years, rheumatism in his bad leg caused him so much pain that there were days when the only way he could get upstairs to see a patient was on his hands and knees.

By the time Dr. Bartlett was in his late sixties, his opposition to alcohol use was so intense that his daughter wrote in a letter to her brother that their father had planned not to go to a dinner following a medical society meeting because he had heard wine would be served.

Judge Ebenezer Hoar said of Josiah Bartlett that he was "one of the worthiest and kindest of men, but who always uttered what was in his heart." He not only provided health care to the indigent but was known to be especially kind to Irish immigrants, supplying them with food, clothing, and fuel when he saw a need. However, his intense convictions and frank speech alienated some patients who switched to other practitioners. Josiah Bartlett took offense, and in some instances, shunned them. When he was named president of the Massachusetts Medical Society, he was so moved he cried. And he had quite the sense of humor. An elderly lady in neighboring Lincoln thanked him once, by saying if he didn't get his reward in this world, he surely would in the next. The doctor countered with, "By faith, madam, that is just what I am afraid of."

The last patient Josiah Bartlett tended to had an accident right outside the doctor's home. Bartlett was too ill to go to him, so instead, friends brought the man upstairs to Bartlett's bedroom, and the doctor treated him by his own bedside. Eighty-one-year-old Josiah Bartlett died on January 1, 1878.

❖

SHARPENING PENCIL-MAKING

The year of 1812 is best remembered as the time when war between England and the United States broke out, but it also saw the first pencil made in America—in Concord, to be precise. William Munroe made thirty, took them to Boston, sold them, and obtained a contract for more. Two years later, he made 1,212 gross and sold them for $5,946. The pencils were greasy, gritty, and brittle, but since they were far less expensive than imported ones, they sold well.

In 1821, Henry David Thoreau's uncle discovered a deposit of high-quality graphite in Bristol, New Hampshire, and established a pencil-making enterprise in Concord. Two years later, John Thoreau (Henry David's father) took it over. In the late 1830s, Henry David became involved in the family business and went looking in the Harvard library for ways to improve the quality of pencil lead. In a Scottish encyclopedia he found one reason why German-made pencils were superior: they mixed their graphite with a Bavarian clay. Thoreau bought the clay from the New England Glass Company, which imported it for other uses, and soon John Thoreau & Company pencils boasted harder and blacker lead, though still gritty.

Together with his father, Henry came up with a theoretical solution, and then he created the machine, characteristically simple, to make a finer graphite dust and hence a lead pencil that wrote smoothly. Having accomplished what he set out to do, the younger Thoreau moved on to other challenges.

Sophia Hawthorne slipped the diamond ring
from her finger and etched her thoughts on the glass.

In 1843, though, needing to pay off some debts, Henry returned to the family business. This time he invented a saw to strip lengths of baked lead to fit into grooved pencil halves before the halves were glued together. Then he bypassed his own improvement by developing a way to bake the graphite mixture into cylinders and invented a machine that drilled a hole in the wood to slip in the lead cylinders. He also discovered how to make the lead softer or harder by varying the amount of clay mixed with the graphite.

People lauded Thoreau pencils as the best on the market. Henry David Thoreau, to the benefit of subsequent generations, but to the astonishment of a number of townsmen, declared that "life is too valuable to put into lead-pencils." Shortly thereafter, he moved to a cove of Walden Pond "because I wished to live deliberately, to front only the essential facts of life, and see if I could not learn what it had to teach, and not, when I came to die, discover that I had not lived."

❖

NATHANIEL AND SOPHIA HAWTHORNE AT THE OLD MANSE

"We never were as happy as now."
—Nathaniel Hawthorne, July 9, 1843

Upstairs in the Old Manse, a window in a small room gazes north, out over a meadow, the languidly flowing river, and the North Bridge. Here, in her home, Phebe Emerson likely stood and watched American patriots and British Regulars exchange fire on April 19, 1775. Almost sixty years later, Phebe's second husband, the Reverend Ezra Ripley, invited his step-grandson Ralph Waldo Emerson to stay. In the same room, Waldo wrote his first published essay, "Nature."

In 1843, shortly after Sophia Hawthorne had suffered a miscarriage, she stood with her husband at the window in this room.

She slipped her diamond ring from her finger and etched her thoughts on the glass: "Man's accidents are God's purposes. Sophia A. Hawthorne, 1843." Nathaniel took her ring and wrote below: "Nath' Hawthorne This is his study 1843." He continued, "The smallest twig leans clear against the sky. Composed by my wife, and written with her diamond." Sophia ends, "Inscribed by my husband at sunset April 3d 1843 On the gold light—SAH."

Four days later, Sophia went to visit her sister and left a "desolate" husband behind. Her presence, he wrote the next day was, "much more essential than lamplight or firelight . . . nothing has a zest in my present widowed state." Within two days, he received a letter from her that he read "quadruply, quintuply, and sextuply" until he knew it by heart, but still he reread it "for the sake of looking at [her] fairy penmanship." By nature a solitary man, he spoke to virtually no one during her interminable (five day) absence. "Come home soon, Little Dove," he wrote in his journal, "or thy husband will have forgotten the use of speech."

The Hawthornes had arrived in Concord on the day they wed, July 9, 1842, and took up residence in what was once William Emerson's and later Ezra Ripley's parsonage. They rented the house from Ripley's son, the Reverend Samuel Ripley, and it was Hawthorne who named it the Old Manse, using the Scottish word for a minister's home. But between themselves, Sophia and Nathaniel referred to it as their Paradise, and in this old house the couple spent the happiest years of their lives. "It is evident that other wedded pairs have spent their honeymoons here, though none so happily as ourselves," wrote Hawthorne a month into their stay.

During their first summer, the days melted into each other. Each morning Hawthorne worked in the vegetable garden, which Henry David Thoreau had planted for them before they moved in. On some days, "work" consisted of picking a few vegetables. Then Hawthorne "rambled along" the river bank in search of flowers. He sought white water lilies for the woman he often called his "Lily" and liked to color the bouquet with blue pickerel flowers and an occasional cardinal blossom. After presenting his wife with the daily gift, Nathaniel retreated to his study, to read "perchance to scribble in [his] journal (or, possibly, sleep!)" He and Sophia sometimes walked together after a midday meal. At night, he looked back at having spent "a day in what the world would call idleness, and for which I can myself suggest no more appropriate epithet; and which, nevertheless, I cannot feel to have been spent amiss." In time, he bought a boat from Thoreau and began to mix exploration of the quiet banks of the rivers with his walks about Concord. Occasional visitors crossed their hearth—Ralph Waldo Emerson, Thoreau, Margaret Fuller, Ellery Channing, and Elizabeth Hoar among them. But mainly, Hawthorne was content to be alone with his beloved Sophia.

During his three-year stay at the Old Manse, Nathaniel Hawthorne wrote "for bread," as he put it, contributing seven or eight pieces to magazines. Sometimes he earned just enough to "suffice for our immediate wants," but there were periods when periodicals were slow to pay and the Hawthornes had to borrow money to pay their rent.

On a winter's day, having completed a piece of art, Sophia stood, diamond ring in hand once more, at the dining room window and etched "Endymion painted in this room—finished January 20 1844." And after an ice storm a year later, with her firstborn braced against her chest, she inscribed, "Una Hawthorne stood on this window sill January 22d 1845 while the trees were all glass chandeliers—a goodly show which she liked much tho' only ten months old."

By the summer of 1845, carpenters appeared at the Old Manse to renovate the house, as the Ripleys had notified the Hawthornes that they planned to return in the fall. "We gathered up our household goods," wrote Hawthorne, "drank a farewell cup of tea in our pleasant little breakfast room . . . and passed forth between the tall stone gateposts as uncertain as the wandering Arabs where our tent might next be pitched."

Visitors to the Old Manse today may view the etchings on the window panes as precious; however, according to Edward Simmons, upon their return, his grandparents Samuel and Sarah

Ripley viewed them as "a horrible defacement of the house—especially as they had had some difficulty in collecting the rent."

In 1852, following publication of *The Scarlet Letter* and *The House of the Seven Gables*, the Hawthorne family came back to Concord. Soon, though, Hawthorne accepted a position as U.S. consul in Liverpool, England. When they returned for the last time in 1860, the author's health was declining precipitously, and in 1864 he died. Nathaniel Hawthorne lies buried on Authors' Ridge in Sleepy Hollow Cemetery in Concord.

THE RAILROAD AND THE MEN WHO BROUGHT IT

Alongside a cove of Walden Pond, a hamlet of shanties stood nestled among trees. Rough boards stuck out jaggedly on the huts' corners, and earth was piled up against the walls of several as insulation. Sunlight mingled with leaf shadows and fell just inside doorways, providing the only source of light. Rough benches served as chairs, beds lay on the floor, and chickens walked around "like members of the family," according to Thoreau.

In the early 1840s, as railroad service extended from Boston into the countryside, the Irish immigrants who laid the tracks built shelters for themselves and their families along the route. Some stayed after the tracks continued on, working as domestic servants and field hands; others moved with the railroad construction. Concordians watched cautiously and somewhat fearfully. Many deplored the fifteen- and sixteen-hour days the Irishmen labored, for what Judge Hoar deemed "starvation wages." In contrast, as early as 1841, Ralph Waldo Emerson wrote in his journal that while the Irish were very hard working, they were "neither the most moral nor the most intelligent." The exceedingly long hours the Irish labored, he noted two years later, "is a better police than the Sheriff and his deputies to let off the peccant humours." Thoreau, who visited quite often with the Irish shanty-dwellers at Walden, found them honest and hard working, but their superstitions annoyed him. After trying to work with one man, he wrote, "These Irishmen have no heads. Let me inquire strictly into a man's descent, and if his remotest ancestors were Erse, let me not have him to help me survey." Others resented the willingness of the Irish to work for any wage, thus taking jobs away from natives. But, of course, many were happy to employ them at those low wages. The poverty of the Irish escaped no one, and Emerson seems to have felt their envy or perhaps a tweak of conscience when in 1843 he penned, "every poor Irishman that goes by and looks over my fence, accuses me."

The influx of Irish immigrants brought change to Concord, and, inevitably, despite its quiet inauguration, so did the railroad, which they had built. On June 21, 1844, with no more fanfare than for the birth of a calf, the *Concord Freeman* devoted one paragraph to the arrival of the railroad in Concord. The train would run four times a day, it said, covering twenty miles to Boston in less than an hour (a significant improvement over the two-and-a-half-hour stagecoach ride). "The cars are large, roomy, and extremely handsome . . . and the conductors gentlemen of great politeness and intelligence." The cost: 50 cents (25 cents less than the stage).

Predictably, stagecoach service, business at the taverns along their routes, and work for related artisans, such as smithies and harness makers, all declined. On the other hand, manufacturing benefited from the cheap and fast transportation, and Concord's farmers had a significantly expanded market for their produce.

The intrusion of both tracks and train into bucolic Concord appears to have been calmly accepted. One writer notes that townspeople began to tell time according to the sound of the train whistles as the locomotives came through. Thoreau vacillated. In his journal, he described "the railroad [as] perhaps our pleasantest and wildest road. It only makes deep cuts into and through the hills. On it are no houses nor foot-travellers. The travel on it does not disturb me." And the train: "The cars do not make much noise, or else I am used to it; and now whizzes the boiling, sizzling kettle by me, in which the passengers make me think of potatoes."

But in *Walden*, he wrote of "That devilish Iron Horse, whose ear-rending neigh is heard throughout the town . . ."

The train allowed men to live in Concord but to work in the city just as many continue to do 160 years later. Finally, it brought visitors and tourists to town. Some came for a weekend; others boarded for weeks. Later in the nineteenth century, when additional lines ran through Concord and created what became known as Concord Junction, tourists from New York, among others, on their way to the White Mountains of New Hampshire, disembarked and took horsedrawn sightseeing tours in Concord. Along their route, they passed the homes of the men who wrote of the people who built the tracks that brought the visitors to Concord.

❖

SQUIRE SAMUEL HOAR

"Walking sincerity, straitly bounded as it is."
—Ralph Waldo Emerson in his journal, describing Squire Hoar

Story has it that after a September gale passed through a town north of Concord, an old farmer muttered, "I wish this had happened last Sunday."

"Why?" asked his puzzled companion.

"I should have liked to see, as it came up along Concord, whether Sam Hoar would have tried to stop it," the old man replied.

Everyone who knew Squire Samuel Hoar knew of his adamant opposition to unnecessary travel on the Day of the Lord. What he expected of the citizenry at large, he enforced rigidly in his home. Times before, between, and after long services at the meetinghouse, wrote his son George were filled with family prayer and Bible readings. His children could not even take a walk outside, let alone play. Their father "held a few simple beliefs with undoubting faith. He submitted himself to the rule of life, which followed from these." He believed, for example, that works of fiction were so detrimental to a person's moral well-being that he forbade anyone in the family from reading them. But he changed his mind when he was snowbound at a tavern one stormy winter's day in 1827, with only a copy of *Red Gauntlet* to while away the hours. He loved it so much he ordered several novels upon returning home.

Born into a family of farmers in Lincoln in 1778, Samuel was a fifth-generation descendant of John Hoar, who had protected the Christian Indians of Nashoba during King Philip's War. He shared his great-great-great-grandfather's principled, direct manner.

Young Samuel worked his way through Harvard College, teaching school during winter months. After he graduated in 1802, he found employment as a private tutor in a home in Virginia and then studied law in Charleston before returning to his home state. Admitted to the bar in 1805, he moved to Concord where he immersed himself in his profession, engaged in politics, and earned the admiration of virtually everyone who knew him.

Because of his reputation, his direct manner of speaking, and perhaps his own background, throughout his long legal career, Mr. Hoar had a remarkable connection with juries, most of whom were farmers. A story written in the *Boston Daily Atlas* tells of a trial where the jury advised the presiding judge that they could not come to a decision. The judge asked whether the problem lay with the law or the evidence. "Neither," the foreman is reported to have replied. He explained that both seemed to show the defendant was guilty. However, Squire Hoar had told them he believed his client was innocent, and since "Squire Hoar always told the truth, most of the jury did not see how they were to get over it."

Citizens chose Samuel Hoar to moderate town meetings eighty-two times, elected him to the state senate in 1826 and 1832, and two years later to the U.S. House of Representatives. In 1844, Massachusetts Governor Briggs sent him to South Carolina on a most delicate mission.

Years earlier, South Carolina had passed a law forbidding the presence of free persons of color in their state. Black sailors, for example, whose ships docked in South Carolina, could be, and were, seized and jailed until their vessel departed. In a number of instances, these Massachusetts citizens were sold into slavery. Samuel Hoar was to go to Charleston, collect accurate information regarding the violations, and prepare legal arguments for federal court if facts so warranted.

Squire Hoar, little expecting any danger, brought along his eldest daughter, Elizabeth. Upon arriving, he sent a letter stating his purpose to Governor Hammond. Southern hospitality did not prevail in this instance. One official after another visited Samuel Hoar at his hotel to advise him of the agitated state of the city, his personal danger, and their inability to protect him. In short, they suggested he leave. Repeatedly, Mr. Hoar sent them away, explaining he could not leave until he had "at least attempted to perform" his business. To one he vowed "he would rather his broken skull be carried home to Massachusetts, than to return there alive having run away from his duty."

For a week the stand-off continued. Finally, on the eighth day, some seventy leading men of the state came to the hotel. The president of one of Charleston's banks explained to Mr. Hoar that he and his daughter could either walk to the carriage, which would take them to their sailing vessel, or they would be placed in the carriage. Seeing no alternative, Samuel Hoar agreed to leave.

The event crystallized his own antislavery views. It also did much to rouse sentiment in his home town and state. In 1848, Samuel Hoar worked actively to establish the Free Soil party, which opposed the spread of slavery into new territories. Within a few years, the Free Soil party, with Squire Hoar again playing a central role, evolved into a new political entity, the Massachusetts Republican party.

Dignified at 6 feet 3 inches tall, Samuel Hoar remained in fine health well into his seventy-seventh year, easily walking five to six miles a day. "He retained to the last the erectness of his tall but slender form, and not less the full strength of his mind," wrote Emerson. "The strength and beauty of the man lay in the natural goodness and justice of his mind." Concord's eminent senior citizen died November 2, 1856, after catching cold at a neighbor's funeral. He lies buried at Sleepy Hollow Cemetery.

A RECYCLED HUT

*"I have thus a tight shingled and plastered house,
ten feet wide by fifteen long, and eight-feet posts,
with a garret and a closet, a large window on each side, two trap
doors, one door at the end, and a brick fireplace opposite."*
—Henry David Thoreau in *Walden*

Henry David Thoreau moved into the one-room house he built at Walden Pond on July 4, 1845, a fitting day for such an independent-minded man. In the months that followed, he worked in his two-and-a-half-acre vegetable garden, rowed his boat, and observed the smallest details of nature around him. He read, walked, and wrote *A Week on the Concord and Merrimack Rivers* and the first of many drafts of *Walden, or Life in the Woods*. He received visitors often and was himself a frequent dinner guest at his parents' or friends' homes. And then two years, two months, and two days after he moved into his house, Thoreau "left the woods for as good a reason as I went there. Perhaps it seemed to me that I had several more lives to live, and could not spare any more time for that one."

And what of the house he built with pride? It too had more lives to live. Henry Thoreau sold it to Emerson who, in turn, sold it to his Scots-Irish gardener. The new owner not only gave up on his plans to enlarge the hut, he left town, too. Thoreau seemed unaffected. Emerson could rent it to a small family, Henry suggested in a letter, or "let nature keep [it] still, without great loss."

But in 1849, James Clark, an admirer of Thoreau, bought the hut and moved it by ox team to his farm on Old Carlisle Road (presently Estabrook Road). Exactly where it stood is unclear. Some sources say it was close to the road; others note that a town map of 1852 shows it situated northeast of Clark's farmhouse and suggest it stood near the road for only a few days while the Clarks dug a cellar hole for the structure.

For a while, the Clarks stored grain inside. Over the next two decades, the hut gradually disintegrated until, in 1868, the roof was removed and used to cover a pigpen. A few years later, its floor and timbers saw new use in a shed, which was added to the barn. When that shed collapsed, some of the wood was used to repair the barn. In the twentieth century, Raymond Emerson (grandson of Ralph Waldo) purchased the Clark property and hence the barn, including boards from Thoreau's hut. It is likely Thoreau would have approved of such recycling.

❖

TRAMPING WITH HENRY DAVID THOREAU

A cobweb is "a handkerchief dropped by a fairy," Henry David Thoreau told Louisa Alcott on one of their many walks when she was young. Thus, in his uniquely poetic style, he opened up the natural world for her, as he did for so many children.

Whether they were the Alcott girls, Emerson's children, or dozens of other youngsters in Concord, Thoreau showed them hidden birds' nests or the most prolific chestnut trees, and took them to the best berry patches. He demonstrated how to make a box for the berries out of a strip of birch bark. "He taught us also the decorum and manners of the wood, which gives no treasures or knowledge to the boisterous and careless," wrote Edward Emerson. He identified virtually anything the children pointed to, each bird call they heard, responding to their what? how? and why? questions in the same way he posed and answered his own. "He was alive from top to toe with curiosity," wrote his close friend Ellery Channing.

Thoreau loved the company of young people, Ralph Waldo Emerson wrote in a biographical sketch. He "liked their informality, their lack of ostentation, their complete open-mindedness," according to his biographer Walter Harding. It is hard to imagine how any child could resist a man who tramped through woods and fields carrying an old music book in which to press flowers, a cane with one side smooth and marked as a ruler, and wearing a hat with a shelf built inside in which to carry botanical specimens.

The findings invariably ended up in his attic room at 255 Main Street, a room that many a mother, regardless of the century, would recognize as a son's room. It was a veritable natural history museum, overflowing with rocks, mosses, lichens, Indian arrowheads and stone tools, birds' nests, one of each type of bird's egg, deer antlers, and hornet nests—everything carefully arranged on shelves Henry had made from driftwood he found in the river.

Close friends, such as Ralph Waldo Emerson, Bronson Alcott, and Ellery Channing recognized Thoreau's genius early. "I meet nobody whose thoughts are so envigorating as his," wrote Alcott in his journal. "His company is tonic, never insipid, like ice-water in the dog-days to the parched citizen." Some in Concord, though, disliked Thoreau's sometimes off-putting manner and the independent way in which he worked only when he needed to earn money. As to his "work" as a naturalist . . . one farmer observed Henry standing in a small pond all day studying bullfrogs and proclaimed him a "darned fool."

Thoreau's way with wild animals was legendary. Louisa Alcott saw him get so close to frogs that he "tickled [them] with a blade of grass, and [they] would feed from his hand in the most sociable manner." When he lived at Walden Pond for two years, he had a pet field mouse whom he could lure out of hiding by playing his flute. In his journal, Thoreau described communing with a woodchuck: the animal let him lift one of its paws gently with a stick, roll it over so he could examine its belly, and handfeed it checkerberry leaves.

Henry Thoreau's closest relationship with children was likely with Emerson's son and daughters. "In childhood I had a friend . . . who wandered in from unknown woods or fields without knocking . . . passed by the elders' doors, but straightway sought out the children," wrote Edward, the youngest. "I can remember Mr. Thoreau as early as I can remember anybody, excepting my parents, my sisters, and my nurse." Thoreau was not only a frequent visitor at Ralph Waldo Emerson's home but lived there for extended periods on several occasions. While the two friends shared much in their Transcendental philosophy, they shared few practical skills. Thoreau, besides being a highly sought-after surveyor, was very handy. Often while Emerson was in Concord and especially when he was away, Thoreau stayed at his friend's house—building, repairing, planting a garden, doing whatever had to be done. And this included, as Edward said, being "the best kind of an older brother." Carrying Eddie on his shoulders, he took the children berry and grape picking. He told them stories of his own childhood, or of squirrels, muskrats, and hawks, a duel between turtles or the battle of red and black ants. He even performed magic tricks.

On one berry-picking expedition, Eddie spilled his whole basketfull of berries and was inconsolable. Thoreau crouched down next to him, put his arm around his shoulder, and explained that some berries needed to fall on the ground so that new bushes could grow, and that, in time, when Eddie returned to that spot, he would see just that.

In 1862, as tuberculosis robbed Thoreau of his strength, he was unable to leave his home at all. The days of ten-to-twenty-mile walks lived on in his and his companions' memories and in his prolific writings. Friends came to him, and he welcomed visits from children as much as from adults. He died in early May, and Bronson Alcott, then superintendent of schools, instructed teachers to dismiss students on the day of the funeral. The church bell tolled forty-four times, once for each year of his life. Many children attended the service, and more than three hundred walked in the procession following his casket.

In his eulogy, Ralph Waldo Emerson told the mourners:

> The country knows not yet, or in the least part, how great a son it has lost. It seems an injury that he should leave in the midst of his broken task, which none else can finish. . . . Wherever there is knowledge, wherever there is virtue, wherever there is beauty, he will find a home.

❖

ABOLITIONISTS AT WORK

*If a statute is passed which any citizen, examining his
duty by the best light which God has given him . . . believes
to be wicked, and which . . . he thinks he ought to disobey,
unquestionably he ought to disobey that statute.*
—Henry David Thoreau in "Civil Disobedience"

—m—

At three o'clock in the morning, Mary Merrick Brooks lay in bed,
suddenly awake. Had the wind rattled a pane? The knock came
again, and this time there was no mistaking its origin. Shivering in
the February cold, she hurried downstairs and opened the door.
Blacksmith Francis Bigelow spoke in his usual code: Mrs. Brooks
was to come quickly; his wife had taken sick. Mary Brooks dressed
speedily and was ready to run across the street to her neighbors'
home, but this time Nathan Brooks insisted he would accompany
his wife, concerned perhaps about the hour or the frequency of his
neighbor's illnesses.

Together they entered the Bigelows' house. There stood fugitive
slave Shadrack. In February 1850, Shadrack was the first black
man arrested in New England under the newly enacted Fugitive
Slave Law. When his lawyer's attempt at obtaining a writ of habeas
corpus failed, several black men whisked Shadrack out of the
courtroom before anyone could gather his wits. After finding
refuge for him at Reverend Lovejoy's home in Cambridge, members of the Underground Railroad drove the former slave to one of
the primary safe houses in Concord—the Bigelows'.

No one but Mary and Nathan Brooks knew how much the
prominent lawyer was aware of his wife's clandestine activities. It
was certainly no secret that she was one of the founders in 1837
of the Women's Anti-Slavery Society of Concord, which boasted
seventy members in its peak years. She served as its president and
chief organizer. Tradition has it that Mary Brooks acted as a sta-

On this frigid night, well-respected attorney Nathan Brooks
took one look at Shadrack's torn and wet clothes, removed
his own coat and hat, and handed them to the black man.

tionmaster on the Underground Railroad and hid escaping slaves in her home (which stood where the Concord Free Public Library now does). Once, story has it, she hid three people in her kitchen, probably in a built-out chimney. Anyone attempting to aid a fugitive was subject to a thousand-dollar fine, six months' imprisonment, and another thousand dollars in civil damages payable to the slave's owner. As a well-respected attorney, Nathan Brooks could not be caught violating the law.

Yet on this frigid winter night, Nathan Brooks took one look at Shadrack's torn and wet clothes, removed his own coat and hat, and handed them to the black man. Mr. Bigelow drove the fugitive in a wagon to Sudbury, where he boarded a train to Fitchburg. In time, news from Montreal reached Concord that Shadrack had opened a saloon there and was doing well.

Mrs. Brooks had worked for years to abolish slavery. Together with other members—Lydian and Ellen Emerson, Abigail Alcott, Cynthia and Sophia Thoreau, Harriet Stowe, among them—she had arranged fund-raisers such as tea and dancing parties and an antislavery fair. Two years after they had formed, the Concord women contributed more money to William Lloyd Garrison's efforts and related abolitionist activities than any other local society in New England. In at least one instance, they raised money to buy the freedom of a slave.

At virtually every tea held for the abolitionist cause, Mary Brooks served her cake, which she also sold to neighbors and friends. Two loaves of the Brooks Cake, as it came to be known, could be made from one pound flour, one pound sugar, half a pound butter, four eggs, one cup milk, one teaspoon soda, half a teaspoon cream of tartar, and half a pound of currants.

In 1844, Mary Brooks arranged for Ralph Waldo Emerson to give his first impassioned speech against slavery in Concord, in celebration of slaves' emancipation in the West Indies. Not wanting to suggest support for the contentious cause, town selectmen refused to ring the bell in the Town House summoning people to the lecture. Henry David Thoreau rang it anyway. He and his family were among the most active abolitionists in town, often providing shelter for fugitives. Thoreau took them to the quieter West Fitchburg station to board a train and sometimes escorted former slaves further.

While Concord's support for the abolitionist cause was vocal and crossed class distinctions, the issue was controversial, as the selectmen's actions suggest. In his reminiscences, William Henry Hunt writes, "my father, as far back as I can recollect, was a strong and consistent anti-slavery supporter and always ready to maintain his opinions . . . [but] in those days anti-slavery sentiments were not popular. I do not know in what way my father first became interested in the cause, my impression is that he was the first farmer in the neighborhood to become interested in it. . . . The troublesome question invaded our peaceful neighborhood and caused more division than anything that had arisen before."

❖

THE CONCORD GRAPE

The creator of the Concord grape was a gold-beater by training. Though an able student, Ephraim Wales Bull was unable to continue his formal education and instead apprenticed in Boston, learning how to thin sheets of gold for use by gilders and bookbinders.

He moved from Boston to Concord in the mid-1830s and bought a house on Lexington Road. Only three trees grew on the property at the time: two elms and a cherry. Over the years, Bull continued his work with gold, but his heart lived out of doors, where he transformed his land by planting shrubs, trees, and his passion—grapevines.

He cultivated the best varieties he could buy, but he was also keenly aware of the abundance of wild grapes in Concord: his goal was to develop the best quality grape and one that like its native relation could withstand harsh winters.

One September, Ephraim ambled through his nursery, sampling the harvest. To his surprise, he found a wild grape with an ususual flavor. He gathered handfuls of its purple fruit and planted them whole, skin and all. Then he waited. He nursed the seedlings. And waited. After six years, he found that only one plant from the original number was worth saving. On September 10, 1849, he picked a bunch of its grapes and showed them to his neighbor. The man tasted the fruit, smiled, and announced they were "better than the Isabella" (one of the leading varieties of grape at the time). The black grapes dusted in deep blue were exceptionally juicy and large—about an inch in diameter. A bunch weighed as much as a pound.

Three more years of careful cultivation and Ephraim Bull was ready to exhibit his seedling at the Massachusetts Horticultural Society. He named the species he had developed the Concord. In 1854, C. M. Hovey & Co. in Boston put it on the market. Their first-year sales of $3,200 were exceptionally high.

Within a few years, most nurserymen in the country had Concord grape seedlings to sell, and a number made sizeable profits. Ephraim Bull was not among them. The fruit of his labor had somehow slipped out of his hands.

Monetary gains escaped Concord's grape-grower, but other recognition did not. In 1855, townspeople elected him their representative to the Massachusetts legislature. Later, he served in the state senate as well. In both cases, he sat on the Committee of Agriculture. Later, Governor Gardner appointed him to the three-member State Board of Agriculture, where he served for twelve years. In dapper apparel, a glossy wig, and silk hat, he often spoke at horticultural meetings and fairs and was invited to lecture at Harvard College three times. In 1873, the Massachusetts Horticultural Society honored Ephraim Bull with two gold medals "for the production of the best hardy seedling grape, the Concord, which has proved, after a thorough trial, so universally adapted to general cultivation throughout the United States."

Away from public life and beneath the elegant clothes, however, there lived a man who grew increasingly bitter. His wife, described as a "sweet woman, devoted to her family" left him after decades of marriage to live her remaining twenty years with their daughter.

Mr. Bull lived alone, transformed into an old man. White hair grew around a balding head. He tended his beloved vines in something akin to a bathrobe. Bull developed several new grape varieties, which probably also would have sold successfully; however, when friends encouraged him to market them, he simply grumbled that "there are no honest nurserymen; I shall be cheated."

The horticulturist and his farm declined together. Friends tried to persuade him to sell his property and move closer to town, but he wouldn't hear of it. One afternoon, as he worked on repairing a leak in his roof, he slid off. Injured, he could no longer live independently, and friends moved him to the Concord Home for the Aged. Though he stayed there until his death in 1895, his heart resided elsewhere. Enfeebled as he was, he sometimes wandered back to his grapevines still flourishing on Lexington Road.

Ephraim Bull lies buried at Sleepy Hollow Cemetery. A chiseled grapevine edges his gravestone, and the inscription reads, "He sowed—others reaped."

❖

BRONSON ALCOTT, SUPERINTENDENT OF SCHOOLS

"I think that he must be the man of the most faith of any alive. . . .
With his hospitable intellect he embraces children,
beggars, insane, and scholars, and entertains the thought of all,
adding to it commonly some breadth and elegance."
—Henry David Thoreau writing of Bronson Alcott in *Walden*

Bronson Alcott strode purposefully along Lowell Road, his feet easily traversing the miles between Orchard House and Bateman's Pond School. His tall, slender frame continued to serve him well. Only the white hair hanging below his collar, beneath one of his odd hats, gave a hint of his age, sixty. As always, he carried himself with a quiet dignity that reflected his inner serenity.

Birds flitted at field's edge, but though he took note of their song, he could not tell a robin from a chickadee and did not pause to listen. A mosquito settled on his cheek, but Alcott brushed it away. The man who had been a vegetarian since his thirties, and who wore no cotton because its production supported slavery, saw no need to destroy any living creature, not even an insect.

As he neared the school, he quickened his pace. Children and teacher greeted their superintendent warmly. His monthly visits broke up the tedium and set their minds racing even more than the field trips Mr. Alcott encouraged. For most of the afternoon, he simply sat observing quietly. He thought it best, he explained in his annual report to the school committee, "to inspire [the teachers] rather with confidence in their chosen ways than to interfere by counter suggestions of my own." Of course, he shared a few of those, too, and taught by example.

Alcott's favorite moment came when the class became his for a short while. Renowned as a Transcendentalist, a philosopher, conversationalist, and perhaps most of all as the father of "little women," A. Bronson Alcott was first and always a teacher. Renowned educator Elizabeth Peabody (founder of kindergarten in the United States) wrote to him early in their friendship: "From the first time I ever saw you with a child, I have felt and declared that you had more genius for education than I ever saw, or expected to see." Alcott gathered the children around him, extending and expecting complete respect among members of the group. He told a short fable and then asked probing questions, encouraging each child to dig deep for thoughtful answers. "I consider these readings and colloquies as among the most profitable and instructive of the superintendent's labors," he wrote.

As a young man, Amos Bronson Alcock changed the spelling of his last name to Alcott and reduced his Christian name Amos to an initial. He preferred to be called Bronson instead, all "for the sake of euphony," he wrote. Shortly thereafter, A. Bronson Alcott began to develop and put into practice his philosophy of education. Its fundamental, profoundly challenging framework stayed the same throughout his life.

Alcott believed in the innate goodness of every child. Each, he insisted, is a part of God, and to understand God, the child must understand him or herself. Most importantly, by teaching a child to live according to his or her highest instincts, a teacher can create a nobler human being and ultimately a better world. But the world, and especially the Massachusetts theocracy, was far from ready to hear from Alcott.

Failure after failure shadowed Alcott's adult years. Scathing news reports and misunderstanding destroyed his highly innovative Temple School in Boston in the 1830s. Though his close friend Emerson described Bronson as an eloquent conversationalist ("I know no man who speaks such good English as he, and is so inventive withal"), Alcott did not distinguish himself as a writer. He founded a tiny utopian living experiment in Harvard, Massachusetts, called Fruitlands that dissolved in less than a year. Though far from idle, he lived in perpetual debt, quite unable to support his family financially.

In 1857, the Alcotts returned to Concord to live at Orchard House, which Bronson almost completely rebuilt himself. Two years later, the sixty-year-old accepted the position as Concord's superintendent of schools for a salary of one hundred dollars a year and began, according to his biographer Odell Shepard, "some of the happiest years of his life." Fnally, he could work at putting his ideals into practice. "Reform begins truly with individuals, and is conducted through the simplest ministries of families, neighborhoods, fraternities," he believed. So the new superintendent visited each of the seven district schools and the high school once a month. He encouraged teachers to visit each other's schools on a monthly basis, too. He invited them to school committee meetings, and he held well-attended Sunday-evening discussions at the schoolhouses, encouraging parents, students, and members of the community to exchange views on education and parenting. He also urged parents to visit the schools. "The parent who seldom or never visits the school to see for himself how his children are managed, and to form his opinions from personal observation, cannot reasonably complain of what happens there under the ordinary proceedings," he wrote.

In his superintendent's reports to the town, which in 1861 ran the unprecedented length of sixty-seven pages, he presented his teaching theories in detail. Children should learn to write by keeping journals, writing letters, and paraphrasing; spelling is best taught along with definitions and derivations of words. Singing and dancing should be part of the school day. He proposed a book for the students with contributions from Concord's authors: the Reverends Bulkeley, Ripley, and Frost; Samuel Hoar, Lemuel Shattuck, Emerson, and Thoreau. Best of all, he suggested an illustrated Concord atlas be written by Henry David Thoreau, "resident Surveyor General of the town's farms, farmers, animals, and everything else it contains," which besides serving the children of Concord would be "a model textbook for studies out of doors." A study of geography and history, he explained, should begin with the immediate environment.

Sadly, Thoreau died in 1862 and never wrote the Concord atlas. Not all teachers were able to incorporate Alcott's innovations. Yet in 1866, a year after Alcott's tenure as superintendent ended, the school committee reported that the staff tended "to teach more thoroughly and intelligently . . . that there's an effort, at least, not only to load youthful memories but to unfold and discipline youthful powers." Ultimately, Bronson Alcott's own prophetic words best describe his impact on the education of children: "Good purposes never perish nor come to nought; as seeds sown on the snows of mid-winter, they find the earth and take root in the coming spring-time, to bear their autumnal fruits for the future generations."

❖

FOR THE CHILDREN BY THE CHILDREN

It was said of Mary Rice that she was "quaint in dress and blunt of speech and with the kindest heart that ever beat." She tended former slave John Jack's grave by planting lilies and making sure the grass was clipped. She worked as a stationmaster on the Underground Railroad, hiding fugitive slaves in a closet or the small nook in the attic over the eaves. She was a member of Concord's Women's Anti-Slavery Society. But all this, she felt, was not enough. More had to be done to bring an end to the abhorrent institution of slavery and to affirm the human dignity of black men, women, and children.

So in 1862, Mary Rice, together with Mrs. Horace Mann, wrote a petition, and then she walked from school to school seeking children's signatures. Three hundred and fifty Concord students put their names to the document and sent it to President Abraham Lincoln.

The president's reply, which can be seen in the Special Collections of Concord Free Public Library, reads as follows:

April 5, 1864
Madam:
The petition of persons under eighteen, praying that I would free all slave children, and the heading of which petition it appears you wrote, was handed me a few days since by Senator Sumner. Please tell these little people I am very glad their young hearts are so full of just and generous sympathy and that while I have not the power to grant all they ask, I trust that they will remember that God has, and that, as it seems, He will do it.

The president had issued the Emancipation Proclamation effective January 1863, but until the Confederate army surrendered in April 1865, he was, indeed, powerless to free any slaves, children included.

❖

JUDGE JOHN SHEPARD KEYES

In his autobiography, John Keyes described himself "in my teens, [as] a forward, smart, impudent, mischievous boy, fully up to my place in the world and quite ready to take a hand in anything going on." There is no evidence that he changed much as he aged.

John Keyes attended Harvard College and Harvard Law School. While in Cambridge, he fell in love with the theater and became involved in politics, too, first as a Whig, then as a Republican. It wouldn't be long before he found himself in the thick of national drama.

As a Massachusetts Republican delegate, Keyes attended the Chicago convention of 1859 at which Abraham Lincoln was nominated for president. One thing led to another and Keyes was designated a U.S. marshal.

In March 1860, upon arriving in Washington, Keyes found the capital in a state of chaos, as southern states were seceding one by one and people with rebel sympathies were fleeing the city. The Concordian was chosen to take charge of the president's security. "It was the most dangerous duty of the day," he noted. "Fears of an attack and assassination were rife, and rumors of real war were in the air." The situation was so tense, Lincoln slipped into Washington in secret. Before the inauguration, Keyes met "the long, lank, lean, rough-looking, ill-dressed President-elect . . . [who threw] his long leg over the top of the center table" and told his bodyguard-to-be, "My only wish is to go to the Capitol, take the oath, and return to the White House as directly as possible." After a half hour visit, filled with disarming Lincoln stories, John Keyes took leave of the man whose life he would strive to protect the following day.

During the procession, vice president-elect Buchanan sat next to Lincoln "trembling as if to his execution," wrote Keyes. But Lincoln was "calm, cool, quiet, bowing to every greeting from the crowd." Keyes rode alongside their carriage, shielding the president-elect by keeping his horse precisely between the front and rear wheels, "so near I could have touched him by extending my arm."

John Keyes served as marshal throughout Lincoln's first term, responsible during the war, among other things, for handling all captured goods and certain prisoners, and investigating reports of espionage. He was present at Gettysburg to hear "those few immortal sentences of Lincoln's that will always be his best-remembered words and be declaimed for generations."

At Lincoln's second inauguration, Keyes was present once again. As he was escorting the president to the senate chamber, someone tried to push past him to get at Lincoln. Police removed the man, whom Keyes later believed to have been John Wilkes Booth. Of his president's assassination shortly thereafter he wrote, "There was the fatal fact, nothing could alter or soften it and to come so on the heels of our final victory. . . . But the world went on, Lincoln was buried, the Rebellion was wiped out as with a sponge, and at Concord Mr. Emerson voiced our grief and homage better than it was done elsewhere."

Within a year, John Shepard Keyes resigned from his position as marshal and returned to Concord. He became a gentleman farmer. An intensely social person and one who spoke his mind readily, he immersed himself in the daily life of his hometown and played a part in almost every celebratory event. In 1874, he was sworn in as Justice of the District Court, in which capacity he served until his death at age eighty-eight. He lies buried in Sleepy Hollow Cemetery, which decades earlier he had been instrumental in creating. The epitaph carved into a huge boulder that marks his grave reads, "The Founder of this Cemetery."

To Honor the Melvin Brothers

The inscription reads,

> In memory of three brothers in Concord who as private soldiers gave their lives in the war to save the country. This memorial is placed here by their surviving brother, himself a private soldier in the same war.

In the photo, eighty-eight members of the First Massachusetts Heavy Artillery and other dignitaries stand shoulder to shoulder at Sleepy Hollow Cemetery, including one veteran who traveled from Indiana to be present. They came on June 16, 1909, for the dedication of the Melvin Memorial, which honors three members of their regiment: Asa, John, and Samuel Melvin.

When the three brothers enlisted in the Union Army in 1861, they left behind their widowed mother, Caroline, two adult sisters, and a thirteen-year-old brother. Caroline Melvin never knew the extraordinary price her family paid for the Union; she died early in 1863. For before General Lee would surrender to General Grant, ending the war that claimed over 600,000 lives, the three Melvin brothers would be among the dead.

With his brother Samuel at his bedside in a military hospital in Fort Albany, Virginia, twenty-two-year-old John Melvin died first, of dysentery. His body was packed in ice and sent home to Concord for burial. In May 1864, after an engagement near Fredericksburg, Virginia, Samuel Melvin was listed as missing. For six months his family back home heard nothing, and then on Thanksgiving Day a returning soldier brought Samuel's diary. In it the twenty-year-old wrote eloquently about army life, frequent letters received from home, his decision in November 1863 not to reenlist, and especially his months as a prisoner of war at Andersonville, Georgia. "If I die here," he pens June 4, 1864, one day after his arrival, "I am sure that we shall die in a good cause, although in a brutal way." One week later: "Tongue nor pen can never describe our privations here." But he tries to, noting scores of dead being carried out daily, irregular and meager rations of mush, cornmeal, and rice, and the almost constant diarrhea. Rumors of prisoner exchanges sweep through the camp periodically ("if not for hope the heart would break"), but each comes to naught. July 5, the day Samuel was to have been discharged, passes. A few days later, he learns from newly arrived prisoners that his oldest brother, Asa, died at the Battle of Petersburg. In August, Samuel's health declines further, and eleven days in his diary bear no entries. One by one, four of the five men from his company who had been captured with him, die.

Then early in September hope flares as sixteen detachments leave. On September 12, he receives word to report to the gate; he, too, is to be part of a prisoner exchange. Another long wait follows at the depot. They board the train and depart. Then, a few miles along the track, the train derails, and Samuel Melvin is returned to Andersonville. His condition worsens immediately, and authorities transfer him to the hospital. "As things look now," his last entry reads, "I stand a good chance to lay my bones in old Georgia, but I'd hate to as bad as one can, for I want to go home." Samuel died September 25, 1864, and was buried in grave 9736.

In the four months that Samuel's life ebbed at Andersonville, 8,636 Union soldiers died there, over a third being held. More men perished at this notorious prison (a total of 13,714) than in the six bloodiest battles of the war. Subsequently, Union officials tried and executed the commandant, Henry Wirz, as a war criminal.

One prisoner of war in Samuel's company survived—Lucius Wilder who, forty-five years later, came over one thousand miles from Indiana to pay tribute to his friend and all who lost their lives in the war. Lucius came a long way, while the surviving brother, James, waited a long time. In the last year of the war, James had joined the Sixth Regiment. In 1865, at war's end, he was only seventeen and penniless. He vowed, though, someday to honor his brothers. A few years after Daniel Chester French created Concord's Minute Man statue, James first consulted with his friend. Twenty-five years later, he finally had the funds to pay him.

French crafted a seven-foot marble statue of Victory in mourning. In her right hand she lifts folds of the American flag, in her left she holds a laurel branch. Her sorrow-filled eyes look down upon three simple dark slate tablets, each inlaid with a musket and wreath of bronze and the name, date, and place where Asa, John, and Samuel died. Mountain laurels, rhododendrons, and hemlocks provide a perennial green backdrop, while the memorial symbolically honors all who died in the Civil War from disease, deprivation, or battlefield wounds.

In 1915, six years after the dedication, James Melvin died. He lies buried next to his parents and brother John on a ridge at Sleepy Hollow, a short walk from the memorial.

❖

The Blizzard of 1867

Immediately after a winter storm, farmers would tip their sleds upside down, attach them to a team of oxen or horses, and force their way through the snow to the center of town, where delighted tavernkeepers thanked them with a mug of hot flip. In this way, townspeople had a smooth packed path over which to run their sleighs. The storm of January 1867, however, dumped so much snow on Concord it took six horse teams four hours to break out a three mile stretch of road.

The storm completely reshaped the contours of the land. Had one youngster balanced on another's shoulders, he still could not have reached the top of the ten-foot drifts on the Milldam. And it provided excitement for all. Children took time away from spectacular sledding to join the adults of the town in watching Mr. Bean take advantage of slick roads. He had twenty-two yoke of oxen slide a house to a new location down Main Street.

Unfortunately mucky mud follows sparkling snow as surely as spring follows winter. After the thaw, one Concord resident wrote,

"Mud prevails and reigns on the roads, mud seems now the mark of distinction. Everybody wears it on some part of their personage or equipage."

❖

CONCORD'S MILL

"Dom it, that is good cloth; it will sell," said the sales agent in Boston, and this is how, tradition has it, Calvin Damon's new cloth—domett—got its name. And sell it did. The flannel cloth, manufactured in Damon's mill along the Assabet River, had a cotton warp and wool filling and served as an excellent substitute for linsey-woolsey.

The Concord mill was one of the first cotton mills in the country, built in 1808, under different ownership. When Calvin Damon purchased it in 1834, he brought with him years of mill experience. Besides introducing the new cloth, he also raised the height of the mill dam and built a more efficient wheel. His business flourished, and Damon Mill, under various names and partnerships, was Concord's largest employer for most of the rest of the nineteenth century.

Calvin Damon died young, in 1854, and his seventeen-year-old eldest son, Edward, took over the running of the mill. Under his father's guidance, he had already worked in several capacities, and he would continue to be involved in virtually every aspect of the mill's operation through his forty-five years at the helm.

The Civil War brought huge orders from the Union army, but production came to a complete halt in June 1862 when fire destroyed the building. Construction on an expanded, state-of-the-art replacement began immediately, and soon the deafening clatter of working looms resounded off the walls of the new three-story brick building. In 1865, Damon Mill converted 40,000 pounds of cotton into 566,000 yards of cloth, sold all over the country. Over the next few years, Damon added buildings and converted others. He also built more multifamily homes for employees, whose number averaged 100 but during peak production years rose as high as 175. A company store opened for their convenience since the mill stood miles from the center of town.

Despite temporary setbacks, such as the 1876 flood, which damaged the dam, waste gates, and some housing, Damondale Mill, as it was now known, provided its owners with a healthy income. By the latter part of the century, it expanded its line to 150 types of woven goods, including flannels, serges, cords, fine worsteds, shirting, and tweeds, more than doubling its Civil War production to 1,250,000 yards of fabric.

Half male, half female, the ranks of the workers were a mix of Yankees and Irish, and a small number of Canadians and Scots. Edward Damon had a reputation as a hands-on employer. Some complained that he supervised work too closely while others recognized that he simply expected of his employees the same hard work he himself devoted to the mill. Though workers apparently never went on strike, individually or in small groups they periodically protested against low pay or refused to work overtime.

Damon involved himself in his employees' lives outside the mill almost as much as inside. He was known, on occasion, to take drunks home or, if they were belligerent, to arrest them. A few he fired for behavior off the job, not on. He kept in close contact with workers' family difficulties—illness or the loss of a child. In some cases he helped make funeral arrangements or bought a coffin.

Somehow, he also managed to find time to serve the town of Concord—as selectman, water commissioner, school committee member, and library committee member. He shared his expertise on building committees for schools and the almshouse. By the last decade of the nineteenth century, Edward Damon's health began to fail, and his son Ralph headed the business though Edward still controlled the purse strings as treasurer. The company never recovered from the impact of a national depression in 1893. Five years later, the Middlesex Institute for Savings foreclosed on the property and sold it at auction. Edward Damon died in 1901 and lies buried at Sleepy Hollow Cemetery.

For a few years, the Concord Rubber Company made raincoats and rubber footwear at Damondale. Then the building reverted to its life as a mill, under the American Woolen Company. For many years after 1923, it was used for cold storage, and then in the early 1970s it stood vacant. Dr. Richard Damon (great-grandson of Edward) became involved as a limited partner in restoring the mill for multicommercial, office, and light industrial use. In 1979, the revitalized building, with Damondale still distinctly written in brick letters on the side, was included in the National Register of Historic Places. Today, it houses over three dozen businesses.

❖

THE SAGE OF CONCORD

"Trust thyself; every heart vibrates to that iron string. . . .
Nothing is at last sacred but the integrity of your own mind."
—Ralph Waldo Emerson in "Self-Reliance"

When the *Olympus* dropped anchor in Boston Harbor, church bells rang for fifteen minutes in Concord. The welcoming committee had also arranged for the bells to ring again—twelve times for the noon train, three for the three o'clock train, and so forth—further alerting townspeople to the exact time on May 27, 1873, when Ralph Waldo Emerson and his daughter Ellen would arrive at the depot. Delays in Boston disrupted plans, and finally, to clear confusion, the engineer of the train that carried the Emersons blew the whistle all the way from Walden Woods, reaching virtually every ear in town.

Hundreds flocked to the station, cheering as seventy-year-old Emerson, Transcendentalist philosopher, poet, essayist, lecturer, and venerated Concord resident, returned from his trip abroad. A band and procession escorted the travelers down Main Street and Lexington Road before they passed under a welcoming arch into their rebuilt house, while school children sang, "Home, Sweet Home."

Ten months earlier, in late July 1872, Waldo Emerson had woken at night to what he mistook for the sound of rain. It was raining, but the crackling noise that had disrupted his sleep was that of fire in the walls. Smoke filled the attic, but no flames were visible. Emerson roused his wife, Lydian, raced outside calling for neighbors to spread the alarm, and then grabbed the manuscript on which he was working.

Townspeople arrived and for three hours scurried back and forth, rescuing everything they could while firemen contained the fire to the roof and upper stories. Men moved Ellen's piano to Sam Staples's home next door. A neighbor covered the flour and sugar from the rain. Louisa and May Alcott gathered Emerson's manuscripts for safekeeping, while others carried armloads of his books out of danger. John Keyes took the Emersons to his home for the day before they could be settled in rooms at the Old Manse. Emerson recorded in his memorandum book: "Our house burned."

The response from friends and acquaintances to the Emersons' loss was unprecedented. "No one ever saw such an outburst of sympathy and kindness as our fire has drawn from the world," wrote Ellen. Even though their home was insured, money flowed in from many sources, totaling over seventeen thousand dollars. Friends insisted it could be used for restoration work or whatever purpose the Emersons chose. Judge Rockwood Hoar suggested a trip to Europe; John Keyes offered to supervise rebuilding. The Emersons may have been surprised by the outpouring of support, but it was completely in keeping with Waldo Emerson's own life-long generosity to friends in need.

After visiting Concord, a reporter for the *Hartford Courant* wrote,

> It is impossible to convey any sense of the tender venera-
> tion in which Mr. Emerson is held by his neighbors. It is
> not all explained by his great fame and recognition of his

majestic intellect; the love for him is a reflection of his sincere regard for his neighbors and his unassumed attachment to the dear old town.

Ralph Waldo Emerson could trace his ancestry back along a line of ministers, including the Reverend Peter Bulkeley, Concord's first pastor. The Reverend William Emerson, the patriot, was his grandfather, and Waldo Emerson likewise joined the clergy. At heart, though, he was a philosopher. For years he had been recording thoughts and reactions to others' works in his journal. Boston-born Emerson came to live in Concord when he was thirty-one years old, and it was here that he did all his writing. It was from here also that he began his many lecture tours across the country.

Concordians were initially cautious around the radical Unitarian minister who had stepped down from the Second Church in Boston, unable to reconcile his philosophy with church practices. Townsmen followed long-standing tradition and elected newly married Emerson hog-reeve: He was to fine the owners of wandering pigs. Shortly, he was elected to serve on the school committee, and within a few years Emerson was invited to join the Social Circle, a group of twenty-five men who met monthly for refreshments and "the solidest of gossip," as Emerson would report.

In the decades that followed, Concord residents asked him to speak at every celebratory occasion from the dedication of Battle Monument to the consecration of Sleepy Hollow Cemetery to the opening of the Concord Free Public Library. His many lectures at Concord's lyceum attracted townspeople from all walks of life. One farmer is said to have attended them all "and understood 'em too." Some, like a Mrs. Bemis, who worked for the Hoars, left work early, explaining she had to go to the lyceum. Did she understand Mr. Emerson? "Not a word," she answered, "but I like to go and see him stand up there and look as if he thought everyone was as good as he was."

Thousands attended Emerson's lectures across the country, excited by his ever-evolving ideas, impressed by his fine speaking skills and extraordinary mastery of the English language. Listeners responded to his celebration of individuality ("Insist on yourself; never imitate") and his provocative statements ("Prayer as a means to effect a private end is meanness and theft.") They respected his absolute commitment to seeking out truth. Many were drawn by the philosopher's dignity and forthright, unassuming manner. At a lecture in San Francisco, for example, when Emerson accidentally tipped over a vase of flowers, he stepped down and picked them up; the audience applauded. He carried his own suitcase, walked to trains, and ate what was put before him. At town meeting in 1874, he declined the honor of having a street named after him and suggested it be named Thoreau Street instead. Above all, he treated everyone with respect, admiring talent wherever he saw it. In his journal he wrote, "I see with awe the attributes of farmers and villagers." He insisted that "differences are superficial" and people "have one fundamental nature."

In the last two decades of his long life, Emerson's faculties faded, and eventually were totally eclipsed by what was likely Alzheimer's disease. In the early years of his decline, he could joke with his family about his difficulty with word-retrieval: "It is a triumph to remember any word." But as time passed, he referred to it as "this vexation," adding, "I cannot afflict dear friends with my tied tongue."

Family, friends, and townspeople formed a protective circle. Ellen spoke of the many who looked out for her father's safety as his "bodyguards." By 1880, he made few public appearances; his one hundredth and last lecture at the lyceum was an exception. Concordians greeted Emerson with a standing ovation and sat in respectful silence even though only the first few rows of people could hear his frail voice. Ralph Waldo Emerson died in April 1882, a month shy of his seventy-ninth birthday. Over one thousand people attended his memorial service, many traveling to Concord on special trains. He lies buried on Authors' Ridge at Sleepy Hollow Cemetery.

❖

CONCORD'S FREE PUBLIC LIBRARY

*"Books are the treasured wealth of the world and
the fit inheritance of generations and nations."*
—Henry David Thoreau in *Walden*

—⁓—

Concordians discuss issues large and small at length and, on occasion, heatedly before they cast their votes and move forward. So, beginning in 1869 when town native William Munroe first started to discuss building a library for the town, many raised their voices in opposition. Too expensive? No. Mr. Munroe was purchasing the land, moving three homes (one to a new location, two back some feet), and paying for the building. However, he also proposed that Main Street be widened at town expense, and that became a source of controversy.

Some opposed the felling of three or four old trees. Others claimed the widening of Concord's thoroughfare was self-serving ("an improvement for a better view of the library building Mr. William Munroe proposes to erect and present to the town of Concord"). Laurence Richardson in his "Concord Chronicle" also suggests that several members of the town library committee felt snubbed because they hadn't been consulted as plans were made. Nevertheless, the town approved the funds, and in the spring of 1872 work commenced.

As Munroe's gift to the town was being built, the library committee appealed to town residents for any Concord-related materials they might wish to donate, hoping to create "a complete collection of the literary, historical, municipal, religious, educational and other . . . works of Concord men and women . . . an appropriate gift of the present generation to posterity." By the time of its dedication, the town's book collection had grown to ten thousand books, and it had the beginnings of what would become Concord's extraordinary Special Collections. Initially someone browsing the shelves might well have taken home volumes that had once graced the bookcases of Bronson Alcott, Ralph Waldo Emerson, Elizabeth Peabody, or Frank Sanborn. In time, library employees wisely transferred these precious books out of general circulation and into Special Collections.

William Munroe not only funded the building, he planned and supervised the construction, encouraged donations of artifacts, established an endowment fund for future expansion, and planned how the library was to be managed. The operating budget comes from the town; however, a separate, private Concord Free Public Library Corporation, governed by a board of trustees, owns the buildings and provides for a little over a quarter of the library expenditures.

Since the staff welcomed the first patrons to its new building in 1873, the library collection has grown to over 220,000 volumes. Many changes have taken place. Dog licensing fees now pay for a dog officer rather than a part of the library budget. Also, while in the early years borrowers were permitted to take out two books at a time, only one of which could be fiction, since 1896, no such restrictions exist.

❖

THE MINUTE MAN STATUE

Ebenezer Hubbard didn't approve of the placement of the monument from day one. The obelisk, dedicated in 1837, stood on the east bank of the river, where two British Regulars died in the skirmish of April 19, 1775. The wrong side, insisted Ebby Hubbard.

The Concord farmer was not alone in his sentiments; many agreed with him. However, practical considerations had triumphed over ideology in the 1830s. The low-lying western bank of the river, from which the provincials had approached, frequently turned to swamp in the spring. And besides, had the monument been placed on the western bank, it would have been difficult to reach. The North Bridge was gone. Well, not exactly

*Sculptor Daniel Chester French needed someone
muscular to represent the farmer-soldier who had
made up the ranks of the Minute Men.*

gone, moved. In 1793, townspeople had straightened the road and moved the bridge several hundred yards downstream.

Ebby Hubbard solved the problems before and after his death. First, he donated $600 to build a foot bridge. The town treasurer accepted the money, but the town took no action. Then in 1870, eighty-seven-year-old Mr. Hubbard died. His will could not have been clearer:

> I order my Executor to pay the sum of one thousand dollars toward building a monument in said town of Concord on the spot where the Americans fell, on the opposite side of the river from the present Monument, in the battle of nineteenth of April, 1775.

Two years later at town meeting, citizens appointed a committee to carry out the terms of Mr. Hubbard's will. In time, Daniel Chester French, son of Judge Henry French, living on Sudbury Road, was chosen to create the monument. Daniel's family had discovered his talent when a few years earlier, he walked into the house intently chipping away at a turnip. "A most excited applause followed," wrote his sister, "as the family recognized a frog dressed in man's clothing, skillfully carved out of the hard vegetable." Later he took a month-long drawing class with May Alcott (Louisa's sister) and availed himself of the scant opportunities to study sculpture in Boston. The twenty-two-year-old artist was unknown and unproven. His work included figures of farm animals and busts of family members and friends, but he had never worked on anything life-size.

French's clay model for a statue impressed the committee, however, and they gave him funds to cover expenses. His services were to be free of charge. In the winter of 1873–74, Daniel French went to work at a studio in Boston. He had in mind a specific person as he worked on his sculpture: Captain Isaac Davis of Acton. Thirty-year-old Davis was one of two Americans (both Acton men) who had died at the North Bridge, April 19, 1775.

Judge French got involved in the project at this point. He visited Acton, spoke with historians, and stopped by the Davis homestead. No portrait of Captain Davis existed, but Daniel French's father brought back pictures of Davis's relatives and of men who were said to resemble the captain.

The sculptor now needed to dress his sculpture in Minute Man clothing, and several friends volunteered. They posed multiple times, but French wasn't quite satisfied. He needed someone more muscular to represent the farmer-soldier who had made up the ranks of the Minute Men. Patrick Harrington, like French a young man in his twenties, worked on Judge French's farm. The wrist, the right hand firmly gripping the musket, the left resting on the plow, and the hard muscles in the forearm of the Minute Man monument belong to Harrington.

Meanwhile, back in Concord, townspeople added fill to minimize the effects of spring flooding on the left bank of the river. They also approved the building of a new North Bridge in its original location. Deeming the old bridge too simple for the upcoming centennial celebration, designers took some liberties with the new one. They substituted a more intricate railing, and midway across, projecting out over the river, they added two covered half-arbors with seats, perhaps so visitors could pause to reflect on the events of April 19.

Daniel French's seven-foot statue, cast in bronze, weighing 1280 pounds, traveled from the foundry in Chicopee to Concord. There, the Minute Man stands on a seven-foot granite pedestal on the west bank, where Captain Isaac Davis fell. He faces the spot where British Redcoats opened fire on the provincials. He stands erect, chest thrust slightly forward, proud with a hint of defiance. His feet are apart, one ahead of the other, for the Minute Man is moving against a force he perceives as unjust.

On April 19, 1875, when officials unveiled Daniel French's monument in front of thousands of visitors, two aspects of the celebration were invisible. A sealed copper box lies buried beneath the pedestal. It contains a history of Concord, excerpts from Reverend William Emerson's diary recounting the events of 1775, coins and postal currency of that time, and details describing the creation of the statue.

And sculptor Daniel French was nowhere to be seen either. Several months earlier, French had left for Florence, Italy, where he studied for two years. Just as the Minute Men of 1775 ignited the armed struggle against Britain, French's first full-size statue launched a remarkable career. Locally, one can admire his white marble statue of Ralph Waldo Emerson in the Concord Free Public Library or that of John Harvard at Harvard University in Cambridge. His equestrian statues of General Grant in Philadelphia and General Washington in Paris were unveiled in 1899 and 1900, respectively. And in Washington, D.C., millions have stood dwarfed by the power of Daniel Chester French's 1919 statue of Abraham Lincoln seated within the Lincoln Memorial.

THE CENTENNIAL

On April 19, 1875, at 5:18 A.M., cannon boomed from Nashawtuc Hill and shook all in Concord out of their dreams. Natives and visitors alike woke to a frigid (22°F) day.

The weather of the preceding week had already caused greater alarm in town than the British Regulars had a century earlier. On April 13, snow fluttered down serenely to cover the ground three inches deep. It thawed, though, in time for two giant tents to be put up. The oration tent, 200 feet by 85 feet, stood on the spot where provincial troops had assembled for their march down the hill. Nearby, an even larger dinner tent, 410 feet by 85 feet, and 40 feet high, was ready to accommodate over four thousand diners. North winds blew so fiercely that men partially lowered the tents to prevent them from flying to Lincoln. But on April 19, the wind appeared to be behaving. Even the Concord River, which had thoughtlessly flooded around the Minute Man statue and would have prevented celebrants from making their way from there to the tent set above, politely drew back to flow within its banks.

Concord expected twenty thousand visitors. Extra trains steamed into the depot from Lowell, Mansfield, and South Framingham. Police details arrived from Boston, Worcester, Springfield, Lowell, Fitchburg, Lynn, and Salem. Throughout town, red, white, and blue bunting and flags by the hundreds defied the gray sky. Nothing, certainly not New England's infamously erratic weather, would dampen the centennial celebration!

President Ulysses S. Grant, Vice-President Wilson, three cabinet secretaries, and Speaker of the House James G. Blaine had spent the night in Concord. The governors of Vermont, Maine, South Carolina, and, of course, Massachusetts, were present. Scores more dignitaries, from legislators to members of the Supreme Judicial Court, joined companies of cavalry, regiments of infantry, bands, and hundreds of veterans in the grand two-mile procession.

At 11 A.M., after the Minute Man statue had been ceremoniously unveiled, about four thousand people filled the oration tent. Two hundred guests sat on a two-foot-high platform, some ladies and seniors sat in a few chairs in the front, and the rest stood, quite likely as close to each other as possible to take advantage of body heat. The Honorable Ebenezer Rockwood Hoar of Concord welcomed everyone, and then the Reverend Mr. Reynolds began his prayer.

The sound of creaking wood upstaged Concord's pastor. Then came the unmistakable noise of splintering boards, and gasps of falling dignitaries and the audience who watched. The platform collapsed, sending the President of the United States sprawling to the ground. With dignity unblemished, Mr. Grant stood up, found a secure spot and straightened his jacket. "Have no fear, Mr. President, gentlemen and ladies," Judge Hoar assured everyone, "Middlesex County is underneath you." Then Mr. Reynolds finished his prayer.

As inconspicuously as possible, workers attempted to prop up the platform, but during James Russell Lowell's ode, it fell apart once more. Just before one o'clock, the president and his entourage left to participate in centennial celebrations at Lexington. However, the train tracks between Lexington and Concord were completely clogged by extra trains. Officials hastily arranged for carriages to take the president on the next step of his journey.

Concord commemorations continued. While the centennial committee had planned to serve a cold luncheon in the dinner tent, nature provided a frozen meal instead. Everyone "finished" eating within a half hour. Speeches continued for an additional three hours, though, to an audience in danger of frostbite. The wind roused itself and decided to participate in the festivities. A sky the color of slate sent down swirls of snow. At five o'clock, with formalities concluded, the people fled to their homes to thaw themselves before attending the Grand Ball, scheduled for 10:30 at night at the Agricultural Hall.

Meanwhile, approximately forty-five thousand additional cele-brants who had lined the route of the parade, well over double the anticipated number, visited historic sites and milled around town. Able to move at least, they were likely warmer than the invited guests in the tent, but they were hungry. Pushcarts laden with breads, pies and the like were quickly stripped bare. By two o'clock, nothing edible was left in any restaurant or tavern in Concord. Famished people stormed the pantry of the Middlesex Hotel in Monument Square, but to no avail. Police threw them out. As the afternoon wore on, the trains began to clatter down the tracks once more, and by six, most of the crowd of thousands was gone.

In the wee hours of April 20, the last of the dancers left the ball as well. Concordians had triumphed once again, this time over what to the casual observer appeared as quite a formidable adver-sary—the weather.

Vagrants by the Hundreds

Hugh Cargill had come to Concord in the late eighteenth century a destitute man. In time, he prospered as a merchant, and when he died in 1799, he left his farm "to be improved as a poor-house, and the land to be improved by, and for the benefit of the poor." In 1827, the Hugh Cargill home opened. The number of people who sought refuge there varied over the years, as did the length of time they stayed. In 1832, twenty-nine men, women, and children stayed at the poor farm, as it became known. Fifty individuals made use of it in 1851, though only ten were long-term residents. However, in 1871, 307 sought shelter, most for only a night or two. As the economic depression of that decade deepened, by 1876 the number quadrupled, and the following year it exploded: 1,892 vagrants stopped at Concord's poor farm.

The selectmen, who also served as Overseers of the Poor, decided to discourage the use of the almshouse as a stopover. The town needed gravel for the roads, so sledgehammers were purchased and rocks delivered to the poor farm grounds. Every "casual lodger" was required to work for his room and board by smashing rocks. The selectmen's approach appears to have succeeded. The following year fourteen hundred "tramps" came through town, and by 1880 the figure dropped to four hundred.

In the early twentieth century, the number of people living full-time on the poor farm dwindled. The last resident lived there in 1953, and after that the town began to explore alternative uses for the old almshouse and land. Selectmen needed court approval to raze the four-chimneyed row house because Hugh Cargill's will had deeded his property to benefit the poor "forever." With the court's permission, workmen demolished the building in 1972. The land has been transformed into community gardens. Anyone, regardless of income, can rent a twenty-five-by-thirty-foot lot at nominal cost. About fifty people a year do so. Selectmen add the profits from rentals to the Hugh Cargill Trust Fund, and each year they dispense money to people in need, ensuring that two centuries later, Mr. Cargill's will continues to be honored.

Women Exercise Their Right

"Tell [Lucy Stone] I am seventy-three, but I mean to go to the polls before I die, even if my three daughters have to carry me."
—Abigail May Alcott, as quoted by her daughter
Louisa in a letter, October 1, 1873

—m—

Sadly, Mrs. Alcott did not live to cast her vote in any election, but her daughter Louisa did. On March 29, 1880, twenty women rose from their seats at town meeting, walked to the ballot box, and cast their votes, as the men looked on in silence. "No bolt fell on our audacious heads," wrote Louisa the following day, "no earthquake shook the town . . ." Instead, before any male had cast his vote, George Hoar proposed the polls be closed. Someone seconded the motion. Townsmen erupted in laughter, and that was that. The women had elected Concord's school committee for the coming year.

Further chuckles greeted the clerk's remark that closing the polls made no difference because "the ladies have all voted just as the gentlemen would vote." Not everyone smiled, however. "Some persons looked disturbed at being deprived of their rights," wrote Miss Alcott, and several women found the closing of the polls insulting.

The reporter for the *Concord Freeman*, who apparently had considerable insight into the women's emotional state, noted that when the moderator announced voting was to begin it "caused many a feminine heart to palpitate with excitement," and he thought their "look of eager expectancy . . . was not unlike that seen upon the face of a person who is about to have a tooth extracted." Perhaps.

It is no surprise that the author who created independent-minded Jo March of *Little Women*, and who came from a family long-devoted to reform movements, should have had a role in promoting women's suffrage in Concord and beyond. In May 1875,

*On March 29, 1880, twenty women rose
from their seats at town meeting, walked to the ballot box,
and cast their votes, as the men looked on in silence.*

she had written a witty but blistering account of how completely women were sidelined during the centennial celebration. "I felt ashamed of Concord that day . . . [only] when the gods were settled, leave was given [the women] to sit on the rim of the platform . . . perched like a flock of tempest tossed pigeons. . . . There will come a day of reckoning, and the tax-paying women of Concord will not be forgotten, I think."

For some years, women had been elected to school committee—Ellen Emerson, Ralph Waldo Emerson's daughter, was elected in 1870 as the first woman in Concord to serve in that capacity. But in 1879, the Massachusetts legislature passed a law giving women the right to *vote* in school committee elections.

On July 15, Louisa wrote in her journal, "[I] was the first woman [in Concord] to register my name as a voter." And subsequently she held meetings at her home on Main Street (formerly the Thoreau home) to teach the new registrants how one should cast a ballot. Unfortunately her hope that "next year our ranks will be fuller" was not fulfilled. By 1883, only seven women cast their votes.

To some degree, Louisa had thrust herself into women's suffrage activity in 1880 to ease her enormous grief at the death of her youngest sister, May, in Europe. Once May's baby arrived in the States, Louisa's life centered around Lulu. Despite her commitment to the movement, her family and writing came first.

In August 1885, she wrote reform leader Lucy Stone: "Ill health and home duties prevent my devoting heart, pen and time, to this most vital question of the age." Louisa had been treated with calomel when she contracted typhoid pneumonia while working as a nurse at a Washington, D.C. hospital during the Civil War. The resulting mercury poisoning seriously compromised her health for the rest of her life. She was too ill to attend the first meeting of the Woman Suffrage League in Concord in May 1887. Fifty-five-year-old Louisa May Alcott died March 6, 1888 (just two days after her father) and lies buried with her parents and sisters on Authors' Ridge at Sleepy Hollow Cemetery.

A year later, Concord's Suffrage League encouraged more women to vote, even advertising in the local paper. Thirty did. By

1920, however, when the nineteenth amendment to the U.S. Constitution gave women the right to vote in all elections, hundreds registered in Concord. Among them were several women in their seventies along with one Juliette Rayward age eighty-six and Abbie Stinson, age eighty-five. Mrs. Stinson had the opportunity to vote for another decade before she died in 1931.

THE HISTORY OF A HISTORIC COLLECTION

Cummings Davis, a small man dressed in colonial garb, stood at the entrance to his Antiquarian Rooms. Gratefully he accepted the 25-cent admission price, and then, bubbling with excitement, he took his visitors around, pointing out one item after another and telling the story that went with each. The musket, he told them, was the first object he had bought for his collection years before in 1852. It had belonged to one of the British soldiers killed in Concord on April 19, 1775. That lantern over there, he explained, was one of the two Paul Revere had hung in the steeple of the North Church the night preceding the battle. Furniture crowded the rooms—china, books, needlework, paintings—all items Concord families had given or sold to him.

For years people viewed Davis as a quick-tempered, odd little man, eager to add to his shop what others considered mostly junk. His eccentricities hardly faded, but townspeople began to appreciate the value of what they at first called his "Old Curiosity Shop." By 1881, interest in Davis's antiquities had grown to the point where he was offered money to help pay rent in a larger space. He declined. A few years later, seventy-one-year-old Davis became quite ill, and he approached the men who had recently offered to help him financially to see whether they might be interested in forming an association, which would take over the collection.

In 1886, the Concord Antiquarian Society was "organized for the purpose of collecting and preserving objects of antiquarian and historical interest, and of stimulating research into local history." Careful legal documents were drawn up, paying Davis for his antiques and transferring ownership to the society. The society also immediately purchased the eighteenth century Reuben Brown home at 77 Lexington Road to house the artifacts, which Davis would exhibit. They agreed that during his lifetime, Davis could live there rent-free and pledged to provide for his "reasonable and comfortable support."

It would seem like the best of all possible solutions for an aging and ailing man. But it was not. As a fellow antiquarian from Deerfield wrote in a letter trying to resolve the differences that quickly arose between Cummings Davis and the Concord Antiquarian Society, "To [Davis] there is little else worth living for. He has put part of his life into every article in his house and every one is precious in his sight. . . . [He] is restive under the restriction he is under."

Davis still considered his beloved collection as his to do with as he pleased. One couple who visited pleased him so with their interest that he gave them a cup that once belonged to Revolutionary War hero Major John Buttrick. The society soon discovered that Davis had sold a chair from their collection, too. Davis claimed "that [the society] have no right in the house and that he will permit no inventory to be made," wrote the society's secretary George Tolman. The society's records refer euphemistically to "inharmonious relations" and a "peculiar state of affairs." Indeed, Davis barred them from certain rooms, and the society ultimately changed all the locks. They also put up a sign in front of the house, stating that the building and its content were the property of the Concord Antiquarian Society. Davis "defaced and removed" the sign.

Seventy-six-year-old Cummings Davis was arrested and confined at the house of correction. There, in late November, he received notice from the society that he had been "removed from the position of Custodian of the Society's property." Less than two months later, in January 1893, the old man was judged insane and committed to Danvers Lunatic Asylum, where he died in 1896.

By 1930, the Concord Antiquarian Society's collection, which had grown from Davis's fifteen hundred objects to over fifteen thousand, moved to a new museum building. A support facility added in 1980 was named in honor of Cummings Davis. The society, renamed the Concord Museum, today includes a wing and new gallery space, added in 1991 and 1997, respectively. In his day, Davis drew hundreds to his "Old Curiosity Shop" each year. His artifacts, including Paul Revere's lantern as well as Thoreau's Walden cabin furniture, are among the exhibits that attract tens of thousands of visitors annually to the Concord Museum.

❖

THE IRISH TAKE THEIR PLACE

At the close of the Civil War, a full generation after Irish immigrants first arrived in Concord, they were still not represented in town government. "Culture and religion kept them separate from the rest [of Concordians of English descent] except for their capacity to labor for the economic advantage or comfort of those who could afford to employ them," wrote Laurence Richardson. The censuses of 1850 and 1860 confirm that the Irish worked as farm laborers, servants, and repairmen on the railroad.

The number of Irish immigrants residing in Concord grew steadily. The town clerk noted these changes with alarm when he recorded Irish births separate from those of Yankees. In 1850, he wrote, there were "53 births, 25 born of Irish parents, being nearly half of the whole number, although the entire population was not quite 1/7 of the whole." Ten years later, his relief became transparent: "Births, whole numbers 43, being 5 less than in 1859. Of these only 14 were born of Irish parents, being less than 1/3 of the whole. Last year 1/2 were of Irish parents. . . . America will have cause to be hopeful." The clerk's "optimism" notwithstanding, by 1860, the number of people of Irish descent had grown to comprise 25 percent of Concord's population. Twenty years later, this increased to 33 percent.

In the mid-twentieth century, a Concord historian would write, "It is not fair to say the Irish were exploited. Clothes, food, and shelter were provided and cash wages, small as they were, could be saved." Over the course of three generations any family could "leap from the primitive civilization of rural Ireland to the lace curtains of the successful family here." Unfortunately, the writings of several prominent Concordians reflect outright disdain for the Irish. Some today might suggest that three generations is a very long time to labor before pulling oneself out of abject poverty.

A number of people in town, however, especially those associated with education (superintendents of schools Bronson Alcott and Edward W. Emerson, son of Ralph Waldo Emerson) worked hard in defense of the Irish. In 1868, the school committee began an adult education program with a stirring statement of their philosophy:

> We have a large number of persons in our village, of
> both sexes, who have come from places where few or no
> privileges of education are granted. . . . It is clearly our
> duty, and it is clearly our interest, to give all such persons
> an opportunity to make up deficiencies which exist from
> no fault of their own. They and their children are to be
> our fellow-citizens. Into their hands, equally with our
> own, are to be committed the fortunes of our country.
> We would not have it otherwise. We are committed to
> the great experiment of granting all civil rights and privi-
> leges to all, poor and rich, black and white, foreign or
> native born.

By 1887, the Irish community sought inclusion in town government. For some time, a controversy had been brewing regarding religious exercises in school. Apparently Catholic parents were instructing their children not to participate because the superintendent's report to the school committee says, "It was observed that some of the children were inattentive to the brief religious service." School officials insisted the exercises were merely Christian; Irish Catholics believed them to be Protestant. Having made no headway, the Irish sought representation on the school committee. They turned out in unprecedented numbers to vote at the caucus preceding town meeting, and when the ballots were counted, their choice, Father John Crowe, assistant pastor of St. Bernard's Church, had a seat on the committee.

By the end of the nineteenth century, 40 of Concord's 140 farms were owned by people of Irish heritage. Their occupations were no longer limited to domestic service and farm labor. They now worked as carpenters, clerks, and guards at the reformatory. One more generation would pass, and in 1922, James Nagle was the first person of Irish descent elected selectman.

❖

"THE BIG HOUSE"

Concord's population swelled by almost eight hundred in 1878. The average age of the new residents was about twenty-five, with the youngest being seventeen and the oldest fifty-one. They arrived by train, for the track ran right alongside their destination; they were escorted to a reception room, and, in time, to their rooms. Each man's quarters measured five by eight feet and came with a sink, toilet, gas fixture, ventilating flue, and pipes carrying steam heat. The "Big House," as it became known by locals, also had a hospital, a mess room, and a chapel to accommodate eight hundred, a library, a laundry, and a barber shop—everything, in short, for an extended stay.

For over a year, locals had followed with great interest the construction of the new state prison in Concord. Now in virtually every edition of the weekly *Concord Freeman*, they read a "Prison News" report and kept up with the name, age, crime, and sentence of each arrival. Most, convicted of various forms of breaking and entering, received three-year sentences. So did one twenty-four-year-old adulterer and a thirty-nine-year-old convicted of "lewd cohabitation." For embezzlement, however, a man earned a twelve-year sentence.

The *Concord Freeman* also listed the rules by which convicts lived; in the chapel, for example, they were to "sit with folded arms, face inclined toward the Chaplain." "Prison News" listed releases, too, never revealing names, so that former prisoners could begin with a clean slate. Escapes, both successful and less so, were recounted in detail. The first, within three months of the prison's opening, failed miserably.

The presence of a state prison in their midst appeared not to faze Concordians one whit. Rowing on that stretch of the Assabet River increased, if anything, as sightseers came to admire the well-kept grounds and picnic nearby on weekends. The prison chapel drew many town residents to services although officials expressed concern that "on both sides the sentiment of morbid curiosity was the principal one ministered to on occasion."

Business was thriving at the full-capacity institution. The following year, the railroad built an engine house, a turntable, and a station opposite the prison entrance. The upper floors of the station building featured a restaurant and hotel. Officers and their families, who moved into newly constructed housing, were welcomed by townspeople. "The ladies of Concord Society made formal calls on [the warden's] wife and their two reputedly beautiful daughters," wrote Laurence Richardson. Just over a decade later, the deputy superintendent was elected a school committee member in town. And by 1902, wives of three prison officers founded the West Concord Women's Club.

At various times, inmates did work for the town. They put in concrete foot crossings in the village, resurfaced part of Elm Street, and built half a mile of sidewalk on Barrett's Mill Road. Surplus from its power plant provided lights for neighboring streets.

By the mid-1880s, political pressure moved the state prison back to Charlestown, and Concord's facility was reorganized as the Reformatory Prison for Men. During the day, inmates learned a trade; tinsmithing, blacksmithing, carpentry, printing, and the making of harnesses, shoes, and hats were among the available choices. In the evenings, prisoners could sign up for academic classes, including basic literacy, chemistry, French, and architectural drawing. The programs attracted interest from beyond the prison's twenty-three-foot walls, too. In 1888, visitors from twenty-seven states and seven countries came to see the reformatory. By the end of the nineteenth century, it was "going on with its good work," wrote Laurence Richardson, with recidivism at less than 25 percent.

As the twentieth century progressed, though, far-sighted programs at Concord's reformatory regressed. Older prisoners arrived, easing overcrowding at Charlestown State Prison, but altering the inmate population in Concord. The trade school closed in 1945. Escapes, riots, and a ten-day hunger strike colored the 1950s. The change in name to Massachusetts Correctional Institute at Concord included a shift in purpose. At present, MCI-Concord is a medium-security facility, which receives newly committed male offenders before they are permanently assigned. Few town residents pay attention to who goes in or who comes out.

TWENTIETH CENTURY

THE TWENTIETH CENTURY

An influx of immigrants late in the nineteenth century continued into the early part of the twentieth, so that by 1910 only 38 percent of the town's population was of English ancestry. Over time, the newcomers, their children, and grandchildren wove their traditions into the fabric of the town and contributed their strengths to its growth. Between 1950 and 1990, development increased the number of residents by 75 percent. With easy road access and commuter train service, some began to view Concord as a bedroom community of Boston. The century was marked by efforts to preserve the best of Concord—the memories of the town's senior citizens in an oral history project; Concord's historic homes, sites, and monuments; and its open land. Concordians take great pride in their past and are equally committed to the well-being of generations to come.

❖

BASEBALL FANS BY THE THOUSANDS

Headlines in *The Weekly Enterprise* trumpeted Concord Baseball Club's triumphs: "Concord beats Shirley in Pitchers' Duel" and "Johnson Saves Day for Concord." On August 18, 1926, "Concord Leads League." Finally, in late September, on the front page: "Concord Wins in Big Fight." After eleven innings, the home team had captured the Middlesex County League championship! "Pandemonium" broke out when Concord scored the winning run, the paper reported. "Auto horns, yells, whistles, shrieks, hats in air, handshakes, and hugs" all manifested "delirious joy."

Intertown semipro baseball games drew thousands of loyal spectators to Emerson Playground on weekday evenings and Saturdays. "If it rained, the whole town went into mourning because everyone looked forward to the Saturday games," said Brick MacWilliams, an avid fan. He described how the ladies would "bring their camp stools and parasols and line up on the base lines." A band played, and, for some games, mounted police were present.

Baseball fever had first infected Concord shortly after the Civil War and raged for decades stretching into the twentieth century. The names of the leagues shifted with time, as did names of players, but enthusiasm never flagged. On occasion, Concord men played with big-leaguers. A local team representative would travel to Fenway Park to see whether the Red Sox or the opposing team had pitchers or catchers who weren't scheduled to play. For one hundred dollars, future Hall-of-Famers such as Tris Speaker, Harry Hooper, and Ty Cobb came out to Concord to contribute their talents to the team's effort.

Apart from the semipro games, teams organized by neighborhoods or church affiliation faced each other. Players in the Asparagus League had no uniforms, just identifying caps. Their teams had names such as the Depot, Sleepy Hollow, Hubbardville, and Holy Name Society of St. Bernard's, and admission to their games was free. Men like Terry McHugh, one of the stars of Concord's semipro town team in the 1926 season, later switched to playing on this league and stayed with the sport until he was nearly fifty.

Love for the Great American Pastime naturally extended to the major leagues. To hear almost up-to-the-minute Red Sox scores, folks gathered at the railroad station. "If the telegrapher wasn't too busy taking instructions for the trains," explained Archie Ferran, "we would get the scores by the innings and [learn] what happened." The information was behind by two or three innings, but that was better than waiting until the next day's newspaper story, he added. The biggest crowds descended on the depot for the World Series games when one can only hope the trains stopped running so that play by play accounts could be passed along as quickly as telegraphy allowed.

❖

FIREHOUSE FIRE

A biting northwest wind blew through town on March 16, 1932. Firemen Harold Carroll and Gerald Finan appreciated the warmth of the kerosene heater on the first floor, which rose to where they sat reading in the firemen's quarters. In mid-afternoon, an explosion jerked them to attention. Within minutes, flames engulfed the downstairs. Finnan leaped from the window, twenty feet to the ground. Through thick smoke, Carroll groped his way to the apparatus room below and tried to start the fire engine; a gasoline explosion threw him from his seat. When Finan rushed back in through a door and also attempted to get an engine out of the building, smoke drove him out. The men escaped with facial burns, but the two-story West Concord firehouse burned to rubble along with the pump, hook and ladder, and forest-fire equipment kept within.

Aid from Concord Center fire headquarters came slowly because some of the town's equipment and men were in Lincoln, fighting a blaze there. Calls for help went out to Lexington, Acton,

Maynard, and Hudson. By the time the first apparatus arrived, a boarding house standing only an alley's-width from the firehouse was beyond saving, too. A row of three shops next door seethed with flames. Firemen succeeded in halting the spread at the building beyond, though its roof sustained significant damage.

As firefighters spread out on Church, Derby, and Central streets, which lay downwind from the conflagration, sparks blew onto roofs, igniting sixteen more houses, one of which burnt to the ground. The roof of Our Lady Help of Christians' Church, one hundred feet away, caught fire, but it was quickly extinguished. Residents raised their own ladders to roofs and used garden hoses to douse embers as they threatened to destroy their homes.

Two elementary schools stood directly in the path of windswept sparks. Several hundred pupils watched from inside, where their principal deemed them safe, while above their heads the roof of the Harvey Wheeler school began to smolder. Twice, firefighters battled to stifle the danger.

The town water supply couldn't keep up with the demand, and firemen ran long hoses to the river. With temperatures below freezing, ice glazed buildings and equipment and made the streets underfoot treacherous. Train service on the Boston and Maine Railroad shut down for half an hour. Hundreds of cars jammed nearby roads, and despite the cold, a crowd gathered to watch.

A little after 6 P. M., the fire was under control, and weary firemen from five communities began to return home. About twenty Concord residents left homeless sought shelter with family and friends. Though the fire caused an estimated $100,000 worth of damage, there was no loss of life. As dark deepened further, a few men remained, still pouring water on hundreds of feet of smouldering hoses on the site where the firehouse had stood.

❖

WAYSIDE SET ALONG THE HILLSIDE

"[Bronson] Alcott called it 'Hillside' as it stands
close at the base of a steep ascent; but, as it is also
in proximity (too nigh, indeed) to the road
leading to the village, I have re-baptized it The Wayside."
—Nathaniel Hawthorne

—⁓—

Fifteen rooms, eight staircases, and an eclectic mix of styles—the Wayside causes many a head to turn. Even more intriguing than the structure itself, however, is the tale of this National Historic Landmark. Few, if any, houses in Concord have so many connections to so much of the town's past.

In 1924, upon her mother's death, forty-year-old Margaret Lothrop inherited the home where she had been born and had spent her early childhood years. An economics professor at Stanford University, she was very involved in children's welfare issues. She continued to teach for two more years, but then resigned to pursue philanthropic work for children. At the same time she tried to sell her Concord home to any group that would preserve it, but they could not agree on a price. The stock market crash of 1929 and the depression that followed made fund-raising efforts virtually impossible. Fiercely determined that the house not fall into private hands, Margaret Lothrop returned to the Wayside in 1932 and began a new career.

Her parents had bought the house in 1883 because it was the only home Nathaniel Hawthorne had ever owned, and it was here that he had spent the last four years of his life. From the start, Margaret wished to preserve the historic integrity of the house, just as her parents had done, but her hope was also to open the house to the public to share the Wayside's legacy as the home of authors. She launched an extraordinary publicity campaign, sending press releases around the country to newspapers, literary magazines, teacher associations, educational periodicals, and universities. For a while, she even ran the Wayside as a bed and breakfast. Guests could sleep in the bedroom of a famous author for one dollar a night and eat breakfast for thirty-five cents, unless they asked for an egg. That cost an extra nickel.

Margaret Lothrop conducted the tours, explaining to her visitors that the house began its rich connection with writers when it was purchased for the Alcott family in 1845. For Louisa, it was the most permanent home of her childhood. Here, Bronson Alcott home-schooled his daughters. From here, they went off on rambles with Henry David Thoreau or walked up the street to stop briefly by Ralph Waldo Emerson's study. In the barn, the girls performed plays. Twenty years later, Louisa May Alcott sat at her tiny desk in the family's next Concord home, Orchard House, and immortalized the lives of the Alcotts and the joy the Hillside years held in her children's book *Little Women*.

Bronson Alcott had made relatively minor alterations to the old Colonial house. He cut a wheelwright's old shop on the property in half and joined each portion onto the ends of Hillside and added a second story to another section. He transformed the hillside behind their home, creating twelve terraces, which he planted with vegetables, grains, and fruit trees.

In 1852, Nathaniel Hawthorne bought the home and renamed it Wayside, but the Hawthorne family stayed only a year. On their return in 1860, Hawthorne contracted for extensive renovations, including the building of the curious three-story tower. The first-floor room in the tower became a formal parlor, the second floor held a bedroom, and on the top floor, Hawthorne had his study, which he also called his "sky parlour." Sadly, at Wayside, the reserved author became positively reclusive. His deteriorating health affected every aspect of his life, and he wrote little that met his standards. The changes to his home also failed to please him:

> I have been equally unsuccessful in my architectural
> projects; and have transformed a simple and small old
> farm-house into the absurdest anomaly you ever saw . . .
> an unimaginable sort of thing . . .

A few years after Nathaniel Hawthorne's death in 1864, his heirs sold the home. It changed hands three times (one owner, a Miss Pratt, ran a boarding school for young ladies here) before Harriet and Daniel Lothrop bought it. Harriet Lothrop was the third author to live here. Under the pen name Margaret Sidney, she wrote a successful series of children's books, *The Five Little Peppers.*

Margaret Lothrop spent a decade digging further back into her home's earlier years and then added her name to the list of Wayside writers with the publication of her book *The Wayside: Home of Authors.* The original house dates back to 1717. A descendant of John Hoar once owned the home, as did the brother of grape-grower Ephraim Bull. During the 1770s, patriot Samuel Whitney, Muster Master for the Concord Minute Men lived here, as did his slave Casey. The latter ran away after an altercation with his owners, hid from the search party in the freezing waters of Great Meadows, and then enlisted in the army and so earned his freedom. By contrast, in 1847 with the Alcotts in residence, Wayside served as a refuge for a fugitive slave.

Deep into her senior years, Margaret Lothrop met visitors at the door and graciously escorted them around her beloved home. Concurrently she worked on entrusting the Wayside to good hands. In 1965, it became part of Minute Man National Historic Park—the first literary site acquired by the National Park Service. Miss Lothrop spent the last years of her life helping the park service restore the home. In 1971, one year after her death at age eighty-seven, the Wayside reopened to the public. In the fall of 2001, the house was among the first twenty-five locations included on the National Underground Railroad Network to Freedom.

❖

NASHAWTUC LIGHT

The Sudbury River flowed by more lazily than usual as Hans Miller sat on his veranda smoking his pipe and gazing at the tranquil scene. The water level was exceptionally low in the summer of

1930, and rocks, which had threatened the bottoms of boats since man first navigated these waters, posed an even greater risk. The rumble of an outboard motor broke the quiet. The unmistakable crunch of metal hitting granite followed. Then came a pathetic sputter, before silence settled once more.

For years, the Millers had tried to warn boaters of a pesky underwater boulder. They placed a bobbing sign in the water, but it drifted away. A red flag hanging from a branch proved equally ineffective. It was time for a dramatic solution, Mr. Miller decided—a lighthouse.

The amateur "pharologist" drilled holes in the large rock and inserted iron rods. Around these, he placed a large cylinder, which he filled with concrete. The rest of the summer, Mr. Miller spent building his lighthouse. He scoured the town dump and area factories for salvageable materials. The Edison Company in Lynn provided switches and electrical equipment; in exchange, Miller gave them permission to use a photograph of the lighthouse in their advertising. Electric wiring ran underground from the structure to the Millers' home, where it connected with their house current. Invitations drew neighbors and friends to the official christening of Nashawtuc Light on Boulder 88. Once the ritual bottle of champagne had been broken, the party began, punctuated by flashes from the fifteen-foot tower.

For several years, the slender white lighthouse worked, but the moods of a river change as surely as the seasons. The winter of 1936 brought drenching rains, snow, and numbing cold. Ice froze the river. Then, as the water level rose, the ice broke apart and floated downstream. The Millers ventured out with poles to try to push it away from their lighthouse. The water kept rising, and huge cakes of ice, no longer able to flow under Nashawtuc Bridge, backed up and pressed against the top of the lighthouse. Finally, Hans Miller's creation gave way and toppled into the water. The upturned rock remains today, scraping the bottom of any unwary canoeist or kayaker.

❖

BREAK A LEG

"I like tragic plays . . . We set up fine ones, and make harps, castles, armor, dresses, water-falls, and thunder, and have great fun."
—Louisa May Alcott in her diary 1850

Stage lights illuminated a scene depicting Concord Square, and the audience looked on as Act I, Scene 1 unfolded: Native Americans received gifts from the first settlers of Concord in exchange for six square miles of land. The Concord Players were staging their most ambitious production ever, "The Drama of Concord," a pageant to celebrate the town's tercentenary, with a cast of 245, of whom 100 had speaking parts.

Remarkably, the cast included at least one descendant of every original settler (with the exception of those who left for Connecticut with Reverend Jones). It boasted exclusively local talent. Among them, Louisa Alcott "Polly" Kussin appeared as her great-aunt Louisa, and B. Alcott Pratt played great-grandfather Bronson Alcott.

Allen French, historian and author of thirty-one books, had accepted the challenge of writing the script. He created a series of dramatic scenes capturing key events and people in the town's history, ending with the Civil War. Then he entrusted the play to the hands of the Concord Players.

Scores of actors couldn't be accomodated in the wings or other offstage areas. Instead, many waited in the Congregational church across Walden Street while others were at the Unitarian church behind the theatre. Heddy Kent worked as "call boy" on the production. Cued by the stage manager, she got word to the churches and summoned players as needed.

Heddy's family had deep roots in Concord's amateur theater productions. She grew up thinking, "First you were a kid, and then you were a Concord Player," and has never changed her mind. Though she has acted in several plays, her favorite work is with props. She keeps track of hundreds of them—tables, canes, goblets, umbrellas—all stored in the theater basement. She searches for unique items, like a carousel horse the Players needed when they put on *Into the Woods*. (She found one at an antique shop in Georgetown.) Her favorite part of the job, especially when she was younger, was placing props as swiftly as possible during scene changes.

Amateur theater productions in Concord predate even Heddy's many decades of dedicated participation. A young Louisa May Alcott, together with her sisters and friends staged plays first in the barn at the Wayside and later in the Old Town Hall. Between 1875 and 1918, the Concord Dramatic Club intermittently entertained fellow citizens. The Concord Players followed. In 1919, they began season upon season of well-attended productions.

One of their most popular is a dramatic adaptation of *Little Women*, first staged in 1932 on the centennial of Louisa May Alcott's birth. A Concord Player tradition, it is repeated every ten years to sell-out crowds.

❖

A HURRICANE LIKE NO OTHER

Without warning, the Hurricane of 1938 slammed into Concord in the late afternoon of September 21 with a ferocity seen neither before nor since. Residents fled to their homes while police led some to shelter in the library. Rail service ceased after the 5:30 westbound train passed through. Buses stopped running and a number of motorists passing through sought refuge at the West Concord state police barracks.

Blue Hill Observatory recorded the highest sustained winds ever in the region—121 m.p.h., gusting to 186 m.p.h. Folks here, like those in every town in New England, watched with awe and horror while around them trees bent low under the flailing winds, and listened as they crashed across electric wires, yards, and roads, baring their roots in subjugation. Though 564 people died in the only category-four storm to strike New England in the twentieth century, Concord lost no one.

In the days, weeks, and months that followed, evidence of the hurricane's destructive force was everywhere. At the reformatory, workers quickly erected a wire fence to replace 275 feet of brick wall, which the winds had reduced to rubble. In Sleepy Hollow Cemetery, approximately five hundred downed trees sprawled among the markers. Some graves, like Thoreau's and Emerson's, escaped damage, but the Alcott stone lay flat, and many others were partly or totally toppled. The damage was so extensive that federal workers were brought in to clean up. Subsequently, the cemetery committee started its own nursery with one thousand seedlings donated by the state.

The lane between trees leading to North Bridge looked battle-worn, trunks and limbs rendering it impassable. Falling branches had broken a section of bridge railing on each side of the river. Miraculously, historic homes escaped structural damage though the properties lost many trees. At Wayside, spruce trees, which Nathaniel Hawthorne had sent from England eighty years earlier and Bronson Alcott had planted, snapped like brittle twigs or were uprooted completely. A huge elm fell beside Ephraim Bull's original grapevine, but the vine stood.

One landmark, however, never recovered from the effects of the hurricane. In 1844, Henry David Thoreau and his father had built a house together on Belknap Street, which was sold after the younger Thoreau's death. Fire damaged the home in the early 1930s, and then the hurricane ripped off the roof, leaving behind a ruined frame. Finally, in 1961, the cellar was filled in and the house torn down. Today, a bronze tablet marks its location.

❖

GREAT MEADOWS

"This curious world . . .
is more to be admired and enjoyed than used."
—Henry David Thoreau at his Harvard commencement

—∞—

A breeze skims across the open water and through the cattails and pickerel weed, which bow obediently. Red-winged blackbirds flit from stalk to stalk, flashing the scarlet and white epaulets on their wings and calling to their ladies. Out on the ponds, Canada geese, usually in pairs, fill the air with their distinctive honks or tip their tails to the sky as they feed underwater. Great blue herons stand regally in shallow waters, far away from the path circling the pond.

Dike Trail, as it's called, gives the first hint that Great Meadows National Wildlife Refuge has a story to share. The wide, elevated trail runs arrow-straight between two ponds, called Upper and Lower Pool, and then continues as a barrier between them and the Concord River. This refuge is not a centuries-old habitat now protected. Rather, one man created the refuge and then thoughtfully gave it to the public to admire and enjoy.

That man was Samuel Hoar, descendant of John Hoar and Squire Hoar. "From his earliest youth, the river and woods of Concord were his intimate playground," noted a long-time friend. And, added a classmate, he "spent every bit of his time down there, and not at school." Despite his renowned preference, Sam graduated from Harvard College and its law school and had a successful law practice. His love for the outdoors never abated, and he fit in fishing, white-water canoeing, and hunting, whenever possible.

Sam Hoar and his wife built a home on Great Meadows Road. These meadows on the banks of the Concord River had been used since Concord's first English settlers as a source of hay, up to two tons per acre. Farmers fitted oxen and horses with special wide shoes, which enabled them to work in the swampy area. A mill dam built downstream in Billerica early in the nineteenth century ended the practice, however, because it raised the water level in the river. Over time, the new wetlands began to attract migrating waterfowl and other wildlife.

Beginning in 1929, and for the next fifteen years, Sam Hoar bought parcels of what had once been Great Meadows as each came on the market. He wanted to create a larger flooded area so that flocks of black ducks, one of his favorite quarries, could find refuge and wouldn't be driven away by the first hunters. Using sand, which he capped with stone, he built a quarter-mile dike from the riverbank to highland. A few years later, with more land in his possession, he added another three-quarter-mile dam.

In 1944, Hoar donated all 250 acres to the U.S. government to be held in perpetuity as a wildlife sanctuary, but he retained one privilege: He preserved for himself and his son the right to hunt there alone or with one guest under carefully outlined restrictions. Curiously, he only occasionally exercised his right, and now hunting has long since ceased.

Within a decade, the U.S. Fish and Wildlife Service, who manage the refuge, began extensive dike renovation and constructed additional lengths. Over time they have expanded the refuge so that it now includes several parcels, totaling 3,600 acres in eight towns along the Concord and Sudbury rivers.

Visitors with binoculars outnumber others at Great Meadows National Wildlife Refuge. They admire the swallows' aerial acrobatics and watch two lesser yellowlegs peck in staccato rhythm at the mudflats, while an American coot floats by lazily—just three of the more than two hundred species of birds identified here since Sam Hoar presented his gift.

WALDEN VISITED AND REVISITED

*"When I first paddled a boat on Walden, it was completely sur-
rounded by thick and lofty pine and oak woods, and in some of its
coves grape vines had run over the trees next to the water and formed
bowers under which a boat could pass. The hills which form its shores
are so steep, and the woods on them were then so high, that, as you
looked down from the west end, it had the appearance of an
amphitheatre for some kind of sylvan spectacle."*
—Henry David Thoreau in *Walden*

By the time Henry David Thoreau moved into his hut in a
secluded cove of Walden Pond, much of the shoreline lay bare of
trees, and the railroad track ran a stone's throw from the pond's
eastern shore, as it does today. During the winter of 1847, extensive ice cutting took place there. One hundred or so Irish laborers
came daily from Cambridge; on their most productive days, they
harvested one thousand tons of ice. Twenty years later, had he
lived so long, Thoreau would barely have recognized the pond and
its surrounding area.

In 1866, when the Fitchburg Railroad built an excursion park
at Ice Fort Cove on the pond, the area was transformed. Con-
cession stands, swings, bathhouses, boats, and a baseball diamond;
a hall for dining, dancing and public speaking; and a cinder track
for runners and bicyclists attracted one convention after another
and thousands of people.

Spiritualists and teetotalers came for annual meetings. In 1881,
2,500 enjoyed a program by the Schubert Choral Union. Four
years later, a new depot and a more elaborate dance hall were built.
Four thousand New England grocers gathered at Walden, and
their convention was such a success that in 1886 ten thousand
came, causing enormous confusion since organizers had only
planned on feeding one fifth that number. For years, charitable

groups brought Boston youngsters to Poor Children's Summer Picnics every Thursday. At Walden, according to Laurence Richardson, they "fed, washed, and entertained" them.

In 1896, fire laid waste to one thousand acres of the woods, including some of the four hundred pines, and one hundred larches and birches Thoreau had planted near where his hut once stood. "The shores of our beautiful pond have been devastated by fire and moths and rude and reckless visitors," wrote Edward Emerson.

Shortly after the nineteenth century slipped into the pages of history, the excursion park burned as well, and though visitors would continue to flock to the pond, gradually Walden Woods began to regain its equilibrium. In 1922, the Emerson, Forbes, and Heywood families granted Thoreau's wish, expressed in his journal over sixty years earlier, that the woods be "preserved for our park forever, with Walden in its midst." They donated approximately eighty acres to the Commonwealth of Massachusetts. Today, the Department of Environmental Management is responsible for what is now a state reservation of 411 acres, further buffered by Concord and Lincoln conservation land.

Even with a limit to the number of visitors allowed each day, approximately 600,000 come each year. They come at dawn and dusk, plunge into the pond's clear water and swim through the sun rays glinting across the surface. They come, beach chairs and tote bags in hand, children alongside to enjoy the beach at midday. And they come, in all seasons, to walk the trails, wandering through the woods and especially the path bordering the pond. Off Pond Path, in a secluded cove up on a sunny incline facing south, lies the site of Thoreau's home in the woods.

In 1872, ten years after Henry Thoreau's death, Bronson Alcott and a friend built a cairn on the spot where Bronson believed the doorway to Thoreau's hut once stood. In the 1930s, though, controversy arose over where exactly the hut had been. Roland Wells Robbins settled the dispute in November 1945. Equipped with a pocket compass, a 98-cent shovel, a few probing rods, and a pair of gloves, he began his search. He assumed that Alcott, who had helped Thoreau raise the frame of his home and was a frequent visitor, remembered correctly. Several feet from the cairn, he found nails, and further excavation revealed the foundation of the chimney. Nine short granite posts linked with chain now outline the precise location of Thoreau's house. The cairn, grown immense as admirers have added their stones, now stands to the side of the hut site.

Bronson Alcott was also correct when he wrote, "Henry's fame is sure to brighten with years, and this spot be visited by admiring readers of his works."

❖

CONANTUM, UNIQUE TO CONCORD THEN AND NOW

Thoreau dubbed the land along the west bank of the Sudbury River, Conantum, taking the name of its owner and giving it an Indian flair. A century later, Rupert MacLaurin, professor of economics at Massachusetts Institute of Technology, together with a friend, bought one hundred and ninety acres and made plans to put up over one hundred homes. Conantum would be the first major development in Concord. But it would also be the first of its kind in New England, contrasting dramatically with the post-World War II row housing being built across the nation.

Roads and lots were to conform to the contours of woodland and fields, and as few trees as possible were to be cut. In a throwback to early colonial days, almost one-third of the acreage would be common land. In place of grazing cows, however, the vision called for a swimming pool, tennis courts, a boat landing, and a community center. Perhaps most attractive to the young M.I.T. professionals, who were the first to hear of the Conantum project, the price of a contemporary-style house, designed by respected architect Carl Koch, was low even by 1950s standard—$11,650 to $20,000 including land.

One more factor reflected both MacLaurin's and the buyers' idealism. Each deed would carry a nonrestrictive clause: owners agreed never to refuse to sell to someone because of race, national origin, creed, or color.

Within ten days of the first informational meeting, twenty-six people made deposits. Bob Nelson, an M.I.T. alumnus, lived with his wife, Therese, and their two young children in Watertown. They came to a decision very quickly, attracted by the flexibility in house design, the financing, and the country setting. "We signed up on faith," Bob explained because the lots hadn't even been staked.

However, to Concordians, pristine land was about to be converted into house lots—meadows and woods where Thoreau had once happily ambled, land where many town residents enjoyed family picnics. The addition of over a hundred homes would strain all town services. In an apparent effort to thwart the project, the water department quoted a figure of $450,000 to connect the development to town water, forcing the developer to create a separate water district. The local paper, reporting on a well-attended hearing before the Planning Board, twice referred to Conantum as a "mammoth building scheme." "Several Concord citizens expressed dislike of, or concern about, the entire project," the reporter added. They feared the development would lower property values.

In April 1952, the Conantum project even weathered a bankruptcy. Yet the energy and vision of developers and buyers, all of whom were intimately involved in all planning stages, never seemed to wane. The houses went up, and another wave of newcomers moved into town. They were not welcomed by some. "We found we couldn't get into the Garden Club," recalled Penny Logemann, "[so] we formed our own." Open to all Concord residents, the club continues to thrive today. Conantumites also formed a nonprofit organization, and within the first decade, members built a ballfield on one tract of common land, followed by tennis courts and a canoe landing on another. Residents hold an annual meeting in January, and receive a community bulletin monthly.

The most visible sign of community espirit de corps burst forth like fireworks in the multiday Fourth of July celebrations between 1955 and 1969. Concord had no Independence Day parade, but Conantum did, including floats, and a Conantum-resident band.

Kids decorated their bikes for bicycle field day, got their faces painted, rode ponies, dressed up in costumes. Participants joined sponge-throwing and fishnet-throwing competitions. They raced boats, tried to out-pitch and out-slug the opposition in ball games, and joined a candlelight flotilla on the river or gathered for campfire singing.

Though in the 1970s, these extravaganzas were replaced by an annual summer picnic, Conantum residents certainly have not forgotten how to host a grand affair. In March 2001, hundreds of owners, past and present, and their (often adult) children gathered at the Concord Armory to celebrate Conantum's fiftieth anniversary. Incredibly, almost one-third of the homes are still owned by the original buyers.

❖

THE PEOPLE OF NASHAWTUC

"Each of these landlords walked amidst his farm saying, 'Tis mine, my children's and my name's."
—Ralph Waldo Emerson

The native people called the area where the Assabet and Sudbury rivers meet Nashawtuc, "between the rivers." According to tradition, Squaw Sachem lived here. Then after English settlers came to Musketaquid and the Algonquians ceded ownership of their land, Simon Willard, one of the town founders, received a grant for this choice acreage, part of which he cleared and farmed. This land of approximately four hundred acres has served as home to some of Concord's most interesting, though perhaps lesser-known, figures.

Beginning in 1699, several generations of the Lee family lived at Nashawtuc. Most noted in history books is Dr. Joseph Lee, the Tory. For years, his pugnacious manner stoked church quarrels, and he made a number of enemies. After 1775, though, the vast majority of townspeople began to snub him, for authorities ordered him confined to his home for having passed information to the British. They urged that the doctor be left unmolested, a suggestion ignored by the thirty or so soldiers who fired on Lee's house. Fourteen long months passed before he was allowed to go about town freely once more.

William Gray, who purchased the Lee farm in 1814, never resided here. The lad who rose from poverty to own 141 vessels in his lifetime and died the richest man in New England, had a foreman manage his property. Men felled pines and oaks, two, three even four feet in diameter. Teams of oxen dragged them to the river where they were loaded onto rafts and floated via the Middlesex Canal to Boston, where Gray used the lumber for his wharves and ships.

By the middle of the nineteenth century, the prized land hosted a "sanguine schemer," one Samuel Wheeler from New York. "He was a stranger and we took him in, who did the same for some of our townsmen," wrote John Keyes in the Social Circle memoir. After completely renovating the house, and building the largest barn in town, an expensive hennery and piggery, and a comfortable carriage house, Wheeler left Concord and his many debts, seeking greener pastures.

A retired sea captain, sixty-eight-year-old David Elwell, moved here next. The first American captain to sail through the Straits of Magellan, he had traded in the East Indies and Sumatra. He brought an extraordinary collection of artifacts from his travels. In 1857, fire consumed Captain Elwell's home and every single item within. Only the chimney and cellar remained.

Later in the nineteenth century, tobogganing brought new excitement to winter days, and Concordians picked Nashawtuc as one of the best spots to fly downhill. Soon, skiers vied for the slope. Each winter, the Shaw family, who owned the hill, put up wooden forms to serve as low ski jumps. Norwegian-born Leif Nashe is the best-remembered skier of that era. Crowds gathered and cheered as, hand-in-hand with two friends, he leaped off a jump!

Around the same time, William Wheeler (no relation to Samuel) bought the four-hundred-acre farm and altered its landscape for all time. Like so many Concord farms during the twentieth century, the so-called Willard-Lee farm gave way to development. Wheeler, a gifted engineer who designed the town's water supply, began to transform the land into a residential district. He put in Musketaquid Road, the first of several in the area, and built cobblestone walls around the top of the hill. The Wheelers showed a commitment to land conservation, too. In 1942, Mrs. Fannie Wheeler donated land to the town at the confluence of the rivers, including Egg Rock, where generations of Concordians have loved to picnic.

World War II brought paper and metal drives to town. Residents motored with headlights half covered. In their homes they pulled down shades as soon as lights went on and stockpiled sandbags in their attics for use against incendiary bombs. And as a further precaution against bombers, an airplane spotting tower was built atop Nashawtuc Hill. It stood one story high, had a ladder outside, and was painted dark green to blend in with the trees. Volunteers manned the lookout twenty-four hours a day, a phone line to Hanscom Air Force Base within easy reach. No enemy planes were sighted.

Following the war, with the dawn of the nuclear age, a Nashawtuc Hill resident played a noteworthy role in easing tensions between the superpowers. Walter Whitman, professor and head of the chemical engineering department at the Massachusetts Institute of Technology, was well known not only as a talented scientist but for his "marvelous ability to get people coordinated and working together in a spirit of good will and optimism," wrote John Shaw in his memoir.

In 1955, the secretary general of the United Nations invited Whitman to head the first United Nations Conference on the Peaceful Uses of Atomic Energy. Three thousand scientists from around the world, including the Soviet Union, gathered in New York. Whitman had insisted on personally going to Moscow to invite the Russians.

An accomplished violinist in his youth, Whitman believed that music is a universal language. At the conference, he set up a music room, and men from both sides of the Iron Curtain came to listen. They found common ground there, Whitman believed, and it fostered feelings of good will.

Locally, the second half of the twentieth century brought increasing tensions between development and conservation to Nashawtuc, as it did to other land in Concord and beyond. Various organizations have worked to protect the river watershed and other open space. In 1961, the Shaw family donated Nashawtuc Hill to the Concord Land Conservation Trust, a private land trust. Time has in no way lessened its popularity. With each fresh snowfall, the hill welcomes revelers on tubes, sleds and, most recently, snowboards. With sizable contributions from Nashawtuc residents, the trust purchased twenty-six acres for $5.7 million in 2000 and negotiated a conservation restriction on abutting land, thereby protecting sixty-five acres bordering the Assabet River. They named the land after the first white man who lived here, Simon Willard. In time, the trees in this corner of Nashawtuc will surely gain the majestic stature that Squaw Sachem once saw.

❖

ROGER FENN: THE MAN AND HIS SCHOOL

"*Sua sponte*"—on his own responsibility—is the Latin motto of the Fenn School, which Roger Fenn and his wife founded in 1929. The words also appear on the Minute Man statue, which was adopted by the school for its logo. The colonial adult of 1775, Fenn believed, chose to confront the British for the right to govern himself. The twentieth-century educator saw each of his young charges in similar terms, not as "a tank of gas in an automobile to be filled by the teacher, but instead [needing] to come to school and develop the habits necessary to get his own education."

For Roger Fenn, son of a Unitarian minister, the two Latin words likewise guided his life. Long before educators began to articulate the concept of learning disabilities and styles, Fenn was keenly aware of the individual strengths and weaknesses his students brought to the classroom. One lad, about to graduate from

Fenn School's eighth grade, had worked exceedingly hard and earned good grades; however, he tested poorly. He hoped to attend Concord's Middlesex School. Roger Fenn had taught at the preparatory school for more than a dozen years and decided to deliver his pupil's exam records in person. Though the Concord River flows ever so slowly, apparently wicked wind gusts occasionally whip down its path, for as the headmaster crossed the bridge, the papers accidentally flew out of his hands and got lost. Fenn proceeded on his way, met with school officials, and talked them into admitting the boy. Four years later, having successfully completed his studies at Middlesex, the young man moved on to Harvard College, where he earned his degree.

Abbott Fenn noted his father developed a "remarkably large universe of friends" during his lifetime. For as long as he was able, Roger Fenn kept in contact with the alumni of his school. His son recalled his writing over seven hundred Christmas cards a year, each with a personal note. Alumni remember him fondly, one writing, "Roger brought such joy and adventure to the process of learning, and he instilled in us a great reverence for nature and all living things, not the least of which were other human beings."

Always able to recognize the presence of humor in our lives, he delighted in how Fenn sports teams had an extra advantage at home games because opposing players would be totally distracted by Air Force jets screaming overhead to and from Hanscom Field. A long-time member of the Concord Players, Roger Fenn encouraged drama at his school, too. On one occasion, he added a skit to a school assembly. The headmaster folded himself into a trunk, which was then secured with locks and chains. A curtain surrounded the trunk for just an instant, and then there he stood on top of it, magically free of restraints. Except it wasn't Roger Fenn but his identical twin, Don.

Fenn School, which he headed with "inspired leadership" for thirty-one years, remains his legacy. There he made real his dream of a warm, nurturing environment for young boys. He created a school that educates the whole child—mind, body, and character and emphasizes the three "A's" (academics, arts, and athletics)

The young woman awoke in the middle of the night, sensing
"a presence in the room . . . some unknown being."

rather than the traditional three "R's". The Fenn approach is reminiscent of educators such as Bronson Alcott or Thoreau and has earned the Fenn School as fine a reputation as Concord Academy, Middlesex School, and the Concord public schools enjoy.

❖

APPARITIONS ABOUND

The young woman awoke in the middle of the night, sensing "a presence in the room . . . some unknown being." Cautiously, Judith Fellenz opened her eyes and to her horror saw a "grayish figure at the side of my bed . . . a shadowy mass." It floated to the foot of the bed and then "slowly melted away." Her body rigid with terror, Judith lay awake the rest of the night, a less-than-ideal way to spend one's honeymoon.

Having always thought of herself as "a fairly sane individual," she let a fortnight pass before writing the Colonial Inn in late June 1966, describing her experience. Innkeeper Loring Grimes wrote back explaining that, while he was delighted to have a resident ghost, he regretted she had been so frightened, because "It is a Concordian's belief that a man should be well scared on his wedding!"

As more ghostly reports followed, room 24, in the oldest section of the inn built in 1716, quickly gained notoriety as the haunted room. An Air Force officer reported seeing an intense flash of light and then experiencing a "prickling sensation from head to toe." This was followed by a disturbingly realistic dream of a woman being murdered in the room. Others merely felt a presence or saw an outline of a face or figure to the left of the fireplace. One woman experiencing indigestion felt a "tingling sensation" begin in her head and continue through her whole body. This repeated itself three times, easing her stomachache.

She was among those convinced the ghost is Dr. Joseph Minot, a Revolutionary War–era physician who lived in the house. Others suggest it could be Squaw Sachem, distraught at having sold Musketaquid so many moons past.

Whoever she or he may be, this ghost is not alone in Concord. Sophia and Nathaniel Hawthorne were convinced they shared the Old Manse with ghosts of former occupants who hid themselves in "dark closets, and strange nooks and corners . . . in the day time, and stalk forth when night conceals our sacrilegious improvements [to the house]." They never actually saw an apparition, but Hawthorne wrote in his journal of strange noises in the kitchen and how Sophia heard "thumping and pounding, as of somebody at work in my study." Someone crumpled paper, and the couple surmised the Reverend Ezra Ripley was displeased with the sermon he had penned.

Unlike the Hawthornes, other residents of Concord have not only heard ghosts in their historic homes multiple times, but have seen them as well. The first hint the new occupants of a two-century-old house on Sudbury Road had that they had ghostly guests was when three members of the family saw a rocking chair in the bedroom suddenly begin to rock. Time and time again, they, their friends, and workmen in the house heard more than one set of footsteps pacing the long hallway on the second floor.

Then one winter day the mother, her teenage daughter, and the daughter's friend sat in the kitchen gazing out the picture window at the snow frosting the trees and bushes. All three saw a young boy dressed in woolen knickers, jacket, and a cloak walk toward the door to the root cellar on the property. Then he "dissipated," the woman explained. Stunned but curious, the girls ran outside. Not a single footprint could be found anywhere in the freshly fallen snow.

❖

ANNA MANION, A LADY DEDICATED TO CHANGE

Upon reaching retirement age, many individuals pursue a long-held dream. Anna Manion did, too. Ever since President John F. Kennedy had established the Peace Corps in 1961, she wanted to volunteer said her son, John. In 1977, sixty-eight-year-old Mrs.

Manion, together with her husband, flew to Sierra Leone. There, Charlie Manion helped build roads while Anna worked at reorganizing the office. Shortly after the Manions returned from their two-year commitment, townspeople chose Anna Manion as their Honored Citizen, thanking her for many years of work on behalf of the town.

Her roots in Concord grew three generations deep, and she considered the town "the greatest place on earth" according to John. She served the community as a member and later president of the League of Women Voters and on the school committee for six years. In 1973, she was the first woman in Concord elected to the board of selectmen. Women in town are grateful to Anna for encouraging them to participate in town government. Anna said, "I just decided I was going to run," and insisted, "I didn't run into any opposition from the men at all."

Concordians described Mrs. Manion as "independent, intelligent . . . an inspiration." "When Anna spoke, people listened," Annabelle Shepherd recalled. Once she had explored all sides of an issue, said her son, Anna Manion stood up "to the essential truth of the matter." Among her achievements, she advocated the creation of a vocational school and helped establish the Concord Carlisle Scholarship Fund in town.

She began to quietly involve herself and fellow residents in larger issues, dedicating herself to civil rights. In the 1960s, she led the way in bringing the METCO program to the Concord public schools. After the assassination of Martin Luther King, Jr., Anna helped organize a human rights group in her parish, St. Bernard's, to offer tuition assistance, tutoring and transportation to minorities in Lowell and Roxbury.

Mrs. Manion's life was like a smooth stone skipped across choppy waters. Few outside of town noted the ever larger circles of her influence because she never sought the spotlight. Mrs. Manion died at the age of niney-two in July 2001, and on the day of her funeral, Concord's town flag flew at half staff. Her remains were laid to rest at St. Bernard's Cemetery.

❖

THE SOCIAL CIRCLE IN CONCORD

"Much the best society I have ever known."
—Ralph Waldo Emerson in a letter to a friend,1844

For the first century of its existence, the Social Circle in Concord, a private club of twenty-five men, had an enormous influence over town affairs. "Nearly every plan or measure was first introduced and discussed (there), and if thought advisable, it was put into the warrant for town meeting," wrote Edward Jarvis. However, insisted Allen French in his address at the 150th anniversary the Social Circle "seldom acted as a body . . . never pulled wires."

Since 1782, autumn through spring, the men have met on Tuesday evenings in each other's homes, as their constitution states, "to strengthen the social affections and disseminate useful communication among its members." Ralph Waldo Emerson said this "dissemination" amounted to gossip.

"The refreshment for the Society," explains regulation number seven, "shall be moderate, consisting of only cyder, grogg, flip, or toddy." Amidst temperance fever, in 1831 members voted to "dispense with the use of ardent spirits as refreshment," but in 1835 they reversed themselves. And by the latter 1800s, victuals became sumptuous. Jarvis describes meals of oysters, salads, sardines, sometimes meats, custards, ice cream, cakes (currant, sponge, chocolate, and cupcakes), fruit (Concord and Almeria grapes, apples, and three kinds of pears), tea, coffee, and hot chocolate. Another hundred years later, moderation prevails once more, and members (not to mention their wives who usually prepare the food) are quite content with three-course meals.

Other changes have occurred with the passage of time. It used to be that any Concord resident could submit an application for membership to the club's secretary. Since 1968, the constitution states that "any citizen of the town may be proposed [by a member] as a candidate for admission into the Society." While the Social Circle used to include a cross section of townsmen—farmers, traders, lawyers, a grape-grower, a jailer, doctors, and ministers, in the late twentieth century this no longer held true.

Inevitably, in a group of committed individuals with strong opinions and a setting where these are freely aired, disputes have arisen. In the winter of 1889–1890, tensions between social reformer Frank Sanborn and judge Ebenezer Rockwood Hoar escalated to such a degree that Sanborn was essentially asked to resign. In the long list of past members of the Social Circle, only Sanborn has the word "dropped" beside his name. Ironically, Prescott Keyes, who filled the open spot Sanborn left, had a "tendency to dominate the conversation [and] caused the resignation from the Circle of one valued member," according to his biographer.

The Social Circle invites no guest speakers and members prepare no papers. In the mid-nineteenth century, however, the men began a remarkable tradition. Upon the death of a member, someone in the club writes a short biography. Six volumes of memoirs exist, providing an extraordinary record of Concord men. Many had no role beyond the local stage, but the memoirs give details about the men and events in their lives that exist nowhere else and serve as a unique resource for writers and historians.

❖

SLEEPY HOLLOW CEMETERY SHAKEN AWAKE

"When these acorns that are falling
at our feet are oaks overshadowing
our children in a remote century,
this mute green bank will be full of history."
—Ralph Waldo Emerson at consecration of Sleepy Hollow Cemetery

"Who the hell is Sheila Shea?" reads the inscription on a tombstone placed in Sleepy Hollow Cemetery in 1986. Some in town were amused. The cemetery committee, however, declared it "vulgar." The chairperson was quoted in the local paper as saying, "Everyone's got standards, and it just seems to me that a cemetery should be adhering to one that is slightly above street talk." The committee wrote to the executor of Shea's will in hopes of having the epitaph removed and even contemplated legal action but decided against it. The gravemarker remains unchanged.

The cemetery, on the other hand, has undergone several changes since its consecration in 1855. The designers of Sleepy Hollow created a parklike burial ground in what was once a favorite walking place of many—Thoreau, Emerson, and Hawthorne among them. A year later, town residents had a "tree bee" and planted one hundred trees on the grounds. One major expansion occurred in 1869, and a few small ones have followed.

Some graves lie beneath blankets of moss or Canadian mayflowers. Here and there, fieldstones form retaining walls. Dirt and gravel paths wind beneath a canopy of trees, along ridges, and down inclines, past the final resting place of men and women of Concord and beyond.

Authors' Ridge attracts the most visitors. They wander quietly past a marker that reads simply "Hawthorne"; the Thoreau family plot, where Henry David lies in a grave similarly reading only "Henry"; the Alcotts' graves; and Emerson's distinct rough boulder of rose quartz. West of this area, an inscription pays tribute to Anne Rainsford French Bush (1878–1962), "First Woman Licensed to Drive an Automobile in America."

Sheila Shea was a first in her own way, but also, likely, the last. A friend described her as "very giving, loving, nonjudgmental." Shea had, most tellingly, "a great sense of humor." Over a century earlier, because of the enormous popularity of Sleepy Hollow Cemetery, voters at town meeting agreed to restrict burial plots to town residents. The wording on Sheila Shea's marker added one more restriction. The cemetery committee tightened the tombstone application process, insisting it have five days to approve or reject an inscription.

❖

THE STRATTON TAVERN FINDS A NEW HOME

In the late summer and early fall of 1992, trailers laden with boards, beams, and rafters rolled up to the end of Estabrook Road. Each turned left into a gently rolling meadow, evocative of Concord's open landscape of centuries past. Here began the immense task of reconstructing the dismantled Stratton Tavern from Northfield, Massachusetts. Over the course of three years, dozens of craftsmen and women from all over New England contributed their skills—taking tagged posts and beams, stenciled floorboards, sections of hand-painted paneling—and, like a giant puzzle, reassembled the antique structure. Original hand-wrought nails, painstakingly straightened during the dismantling, hold the siding in place.

For almost thirty years, the Stratton Tavern had stood abandoned in Northfield, its boarded-up windows no longer reflecting the waters of the Connecticut River flowing past. Birds, squirrels, raccoons, and mice found shelter here, not humans who traveled along the river valley. Hezekiah Stratton, born in Concord, had moved to the western part of Massachusetts in the early 1700s and was one of the first settlers of Northfield. His son, also Hezekiah, built the tavern in 1759, and it remained in the family for over 150 years. In 1974, it was given to Old Sturbridge Village, who hoped to move it to their grounds, but unable to raise the necessary funds, they were forced to sell the building. In 1992, shortly before bulldozers were to demolish the tavern, Anna and Neil Rasmussen came to the rescue.

Deeply committed to historic preservaton, they were also attracted by the idea that they were bringing to Concord an antique structure with connections to the old Stratton family who had settled here in the middle of the seventeenth century.

The reconstruction of the Stratton Tavern on Estabrook Road was not without controversy, however. Many historians believe the integrity of an antique home is compromised when it is moved from its original location. For others, the dismay was more personal. To make room for the tavern, the Rasmussens razed the existing house on the property. Built around 1840, the structure with its many additions was hardly significant historically, but for most of the twentieth century, the family of Raymond Emerson, grandson of Ralph Waldo Emerson, had lived here. Some residents of Concord deeply regretted seeing an Emerson home disappear.

Today, the Stratton Tavern, immaculately restored inside and out, stands back from Estabrook Road and fits comfortably with its rural surroundings. Stone walls border the country lane, and after it ends, continue alongside a dirt trail into publicly owned Estabrook Woods. Years ago, this was Carlisle Road and passed through farmland all the way to the neighboring town—one more example of changing landscape.

❖

A THREATENED MINUTE MAN STATUE

November 1973—"Here once the embattled farmers stood, and fired the shot heard round the world." At approximately 10 A.M., a Bedford High School student read the final line of the inscription on the Minute Man memorial, and his eyes dropped to the brown paper bag at the statue's base. Curious, he picked up the bag and began to walk away while his hand unfolded the top. Suddenly, he stood as still as the statue behind him. The bag was ticking! Horrified, the young man dropped it, ran to his car, and headed for the police station.

Cruisers screamed to the North Bridge, where police cordoned off the area. At the same time, others called for a state police bomb expert. As luck would have it, he was nearby, and at 10:45 he appeared on the scene. Ten minutes later he had the bag's contents scattered on the ground: a box out of which tumbled four sticks of dynamite, a detonator, and a clock. It had been set to explode at 11 A.M. To this date, the crime remains unsolved.

In the early 1970s, tensions over the Vietnam War continued to increase, while faith in government eroded. As the bicentennial celebration of the events of April 19, 1775, approached, town officials worried about demonstrations and potential violence. With the 1973 bomb incident fresh in their memories, the selectmen voted to have the statue removed for minor repairs, but most importantly to make a plaster duplicate so that in the event of damage to the original, an exact replacement could be cast.

On the morning of January 16, 1975, midst complete secrecy, French's Minute Man swung off his base and came to rest in a truck before beginning the trip to Boston. For the first time in a century, visitors to North Bridge were greeted by an empty granite block. On March 29, the statue returned, greeted by fanfare. Girl Scouts placed a time capsule in the base, and a crowd applauded as the bronze statue settled back where he belonged.

April 19, 1975, did indeed draw protestors. Approximately forty thousand people, celebrating the People's Bicentennial, camped on National Park grounds. Though they objected vocally to segments of the speeches, President Gerald Ford's in particular, their demonstration was entirely peaceful.

The existence of a plaster duplicate of the statue had unexpected consequences. The Minute Man has long been the symbol of the National Guard. In 1992, the Army National Guard's top brass wrote to the Concord selectmen seeking approval for their plans to use the plaster of Paris cast made in 1975 to create a duplicate statue, which they would place at their headquarters in Arlington, Virginia. They followed this up with a letter suggesting the selectmen "will be pleased to know" that their lawyers advised them that "a local vote or permission of the Town" was not needed but they invited the board to make "suggestions" and "provide assistance."

Concordians had gone through this before, in 1984 when the Air National Guard wanted to do the same thing, and they reacted with articulate outrage. "Aesthetically and historically [the Minute Man statue] is a singular piece, a national treasure entrusted to Concord for safekeeping," wrote former selectman Anna Manion.

Hundreds of people visit the North Bridge and its monuments.
They listen and learn and then carry an understanding
of what transpired here as a guide to the future.

"Placing a copy of the Minute Man anywhere else would weaken the historic bond." "If the National Guard wishes to put up a statue of a minuteman, more power to them. But let them commission a sculptor to create one for them," insisted historian David Little. Ultimately law prevailed. In the 1963 cooperative agreement between the National Park Service and Concord, the town "retained ownership of historic structures, objects and grounds in the Battleground area." No duplicate of the Minute Man statue has been made, nor, as far as Concordians are concerned, will there ever be!

❖

"THE SHOT HEARD ROUND THE WORLD"

Early morning shadows lie across the grass, and the Concord River flows by serenely, oblivious to the significance of the event about to unfold across its waters. British Regulars, smart in their black boots and gaiters, white wool breeches, and red coats move restlessly about the bridge, still agitated by the exchange of fire and loss of life in Lexington the night before. Two dozen of them have gone ahead to search James Barrett's farm for munitions. The remaining soldiers' job is to keep the road and bridge open so that all of them can retreat safely back to Boston.

Over the crest of Muster Hill, on the western bank of the river, provincials appear. They've seen smoke wafting up from the area of the courthouse and fear the Regulars are setting their town on fire. In orderly pairs they march toward the bridge between trees that hint at the spring about to unfold. Muskets resting against their shoulders glint in the sun. Tricorn hats cover their heads. Otherwise, no two Minute Men look alike. The muted home-dyed colors of their outfits—brown, green, smoky blue, grey—are a dramatic contrast to the immaculately outfitted soldiers. They march downhill, united by resolve.

Soldiers tear planks from the bridge, toss them in the river, hoping to deter the provincials' advance. Then they back away to the east side of the bridge and take up positions. The Americans stop on the opposite bank. A pause.

The British fire a few warning shots. Then an officer shouts the order. The front line of soldiers lowers their guns, kneels. Together, with the next row of men standing behind them, they fire. Bullets followed by two to three feet of flame erupt from each musket. Isaac Davis and Abner Hosmer of Acton fall. On the American side, Major John Buttrick gives his order: "Fire, fellow-soldiers, for God's sake fire!" For the first time under disciplined command, American patriots point their muskets at royal troops and fire. Two British soldiers die instantly and close to a dozen are wounded. The Regulars retreat as the provincials run forward. They jump easily over the missing planks in the bridge, but allow the soldiers to make their way to the center of town without further incident.

On April 15, 2000, two and a quarter centuries after the original encounter, spectators applaud and cheer wildly following the reenactment of this pivotal scene in American history. Musket smoke drifts downstream on the breeze. The "slain" men rise, and a fife and drum band plays. Hundreds of people—including babies waving from backpacks, toddlers on parents' shoulders, teens, and seniors—stroll up and over the knoll. They leave the North Bridge and its monuments, carrying an understanding of what transpired here as a guide to the future.

> *Here the British army was first confronted and driven back;*
> *and if only two men, or only one man had been slain, it*
> *was the first victory. The thunderbolt falls on an inch of*
> *ground; but the light of it fills the horizon.*
> —Ralph Waldo Emerson at Concord's
> centennial celebration in 1875

—∿—

❖

Sources

Alcott, Louisa May. "Woman's Part in the Concord Celebrations." *The Woman's Journal.* May 1, 1875.

The American Notebooks of Nathaniel Hawthorne. Edited by Randall Stewart. New Haven: Yale University Press, 1932.

"Autobiography of Honorable John S. Keyes." in Concord Free Public Library Special Collections.

Bailey, William M. "When the Irish Came to Concord." *New Perspectives on Concord's History.* Concord, MA: 1983.

Benton, Josiah Henry. *Warning Out in New England.* Boston: W. B. Clarke, Co., 1911.

Blancke, Shirley and Barbara Robinson. *From Musketaquid to Concord.* Concord: Concord Antiquarian Museum, 1985.

Brooks, Jane. "Cummings Elothan Davis 1816–1896: The Story of a Collector and the Early Years of the Concord Antiquarian Society." May 1, 1986. In Concord Free Public Library Special Collections.

Brooks, Paul. *The Old Manse and the People Who Lived There.* The Trustees of Reservations, 1983.

Butman, Robert C. *The Conantum Saga.* June 1995.

Catton, Bruce and William B. Catton. *The Bold and Magnificent Dream, America's Founding Years 1492–1815.* Garden City, NY: Doubleday & Co., 1978.

"Concord Free Public Library Centennial." Published in 1973 by The Members of the Library Corporation in conjunction with the Library Committee.

Concord Lyceum records 1881–1922 in Concord Free Public Library Special Collections.

Concord Town Records, manuscript transcripts Volume III (1732–1746) and IV (1747–1777).

Cresson, Margaret French. *Journey into Fame: The Life of Daniel Chester French.* Cambridge: Harvard University Press, 1947.

Diaries and Letters of William Emerson 1743–1776. Arranged by Amelia Forbes Emerson.

Elliott, Barbara K. and Janet W. Jones. *Concord: Its Black History 1636-1860.* Published by Concord Public Schools 1976.

Emerson, Edward Waldo. *Henry Thoreau As Remembered by a Young Friend.* Boston: Houghton Mifflin Co., 1917.

Emerson, Ralph Waldo. *Self-Reliance and other essays.* New York: Dover Publications, 1993.

Evans, Barbara Jean. *A to Zax, A Comprehensive Dictionary of Genealogists & Historians.* Alexandria, VA.: Hearthside Press, 1995.

Fenn, Mary R. *Old Houses of Concord.* Concord: Old Concord Chapter Daughters of the American Revolution, 1974.

Fenn, Roger. *Roger Remembers, Books 1, 2, and 3.*

Fenn School Alumni Bulletin, January 1989.

French, Allen. *Historic Concord and the Lexington Fight.* Concord: The Friends of the Concord Free Public Library, 1992.

_____. "Two Concord Laymen: John and Samuel Hoar." read before the Unitarian Historical Society in Boston May 21, 1936. Reprinted by Society Vol. V, part 1.

French, Daniel Chester. "The Story of the Minute Man Statue as told by the sculptor in 1925."

Garrelick, Renee. *Clothier of the Assabet.* Concord: 1988.

_____. *Concord in the Days of Strawberries and Streetcars.* Concord: 1985.

Granger, Janet and Margaret Andrews. *Concord Female Charitable Society and the Ladies Sewing Society 1814–1840.* May 1982. Concord Free Public Library Special Collections.

Greeley, Dana McLean. *Know These Concordians.* Published by First Parish in Concord, 1975.

Gross, Robert A. *The Minutemen and Their World.* New York: Hill & Wang, 1976.

_____. "Squire Dickinson and Squire Hoar." (In Proceedings of the Massachusetts Historical Society Vol 101, 1989.) Boston, 1990.

Harding, Walter. *The Days of Henry Thoreau, A Biography.* Princeton: Princeton University Press, 1962.

Hawthorne, Nathaniel. *Mosses from an Old Manse.* Boston: James R. Osgood & Co., 1873.

Heath, Anita L. "Five Almshouses in Middlesex County, Massachusetts and their Records." Master of Arts Thesis, Univ. of Mass., Boston, 1998.

Hill, Frances. *A Delusion of Satan.* New York: Da Capo Press, 1997.

Hunt, William Henry. "Reminiscences of the Old Hunt House on Monument Street in Concord, Massachusetts and my Life in Concord in the mid-19th Century." Concord Free Public Library Special Collections.

Jarvis, Edward. *Traditions and Reminiscences of Concord, Mass. 1779–1878.* Amherst, MA: University of Massachusetts Press, 1993.

The Journal of Henry David Thoreau, Volume I–XIV. New York: Dover Publications, Inc., 1962.

The Journals and Miscellaneous Notebooks of Ralph Waldo Emerson. Cambridge, MA: Belknap Press, 1971.

Keyes, John Shepard. *Autobiography of Honorable John S. Keyes.* Concord Free Public Library Special Collections.

Labaree, Benjamin W. *Colonial Massachusetts: A History.* Millwood, NY: KTO Press, 1979.

Little, David B. *American's First Centennial Celebration.* Boston: Houghton Mifflin Co., 1974.

Lothrop, Margaret. *The Wayside: Home of Authors.* New York: American Book Co., 1968.

Low, Alvah H. "The Concord Lyceum." *Old-time New England.* V.50, #2, Oct–Dec 1959, p.28–42.

McCuskey, Dorothy. *Bronson Alcott, Teacher.* New York: The MacMillan Co., 1940.

"The Melvin Memorial: A Brother's Tribute—Exercises at Dedication June 16, 1909." Cambridge: The Riverside Press, 1910.

Memoirs of Members of the Social Circle in Concord. Second, Third, Fourth, and Fifth Series.

Minuteman supplement. Sep. 27, 1973.

Mitchell, John Hanson. *Trespassing.* Reading, MA: Addison-Wesley, 1998.

National Park Service archives, the correspondence of Margaret Lothrop.

Nourse, Henry Stedman. *The Hoar Family in America and its English Ancestry.* Boston: David Clapp & Son, 1899.

Oral History transcripts compiled by Renee Garrelick, Concord Free Public Library.

Proceedings at the Centennial Celebration of Concord Fight April 19, 1875. Concord: Published by the Town in 1876.

Proceedings on the 50th anniversary of the Concord Lyceum, Jan. 1879. Concord: 1879.

"Record of Bicentennial Celebration of the Social Circle in Concord." May 11, 1982.

Reynolds, Grindall. "The Story of a Concord Farm and its Owners." A lecture delivered before Concord Lyceum, Feb. 1, 1883.

Richardson, Laurence Eaton. *Concord at the turn of the Century.* Concord Antiquarian Society, 1960.

_____. *Concord Chronicle 1865–1899.* Concord: 1967.

Roach, Marilynne K. "That Child, Betty Parris: Elizabeth (Parris) Barron and the People in her Life." *Essex Institute Historical Collections.* Salem, MA: Jan. 1988.

Robbins, Roland Wells. *The Story of the Minute Man.* Stoneham, MA: George R. Barnstead & Son, 1945.

Robinson, William S. *"Warrington" Pen-Portraits: A Collection of Personal and Political Reminiscences from 1848–1876.* Boston: W. S. Robinson, 1877.

Rusk, Ralph. *The Life of Ralph Waldo Emerson.* New York: Columbia University Press, 1949.

Sanborn, F. B. "The Women of Concord, Mrs. Mary Merrick Brooks and the Anti-Slavery Movement." A Concord Note-Book, May 1906.

Schultz, Eric B. and Michael J. Tougias. *King Philip's War.* Woodstock, VT: The Countryman Press, 1999.

Sciacca, Jane H. *History begins at home: the story of Margaret Lothrop and the Wayside.* National Park Service, 1995.

The Selected Letters of Louisa May Alcott. Edited by Joel Myerson and Daniel Shealy. Boston: Little Brown & Co., 1987.

Shattuck, Lemuel. *A History of the Town of Concord from its earliest settlement to 1832.* Cambridge, MA: Charles Folsom, printer. 1835.

Shepard, O'Dell. *Pedlar's Progress: The Life of Bronson Alcott.* Boston: Little, Brown and Company, 1937.

Shipton, Clifford. *Sibley's Harvard Graduates,* Vol. XII 1746–1750. Boston: Massachusetts Historical Society, 1962.

Stern, Madeleine B. *Louisa May Alcott, a Biography.* Boston: Northeastern University Press, 1996.

Survey of Historical and Architectural Resources, Vol. III. Concord, MA: 1994.

Thoreau, Henry David. *Walden.* Princeton, NJ: Princeton University Press, 1971.

Tolman, George. "John Jack, the Slave and Daniel Bliss, the Tory." A paper presented before the Concord Antiquarian Society, 1902.

Turley, Janet. "Westvale: Concord's Earliest Industrial Area." 1980. Manuscript in Concord Free Public Library Special Collections.

Walcott, Charles H. *Concord in the Colonial Period.* Boston: Estes & Lauriat, 1884.

Wheeler, Ruth. Articles in the *Concord Enterprise* and *Concord Journal.* Concord Free Public Library Special Collections.

_____. *Concord: Climate for Freedom.* Concord, MA: The Concord Antiquarian Society, 1967.

_____. "Concord Friendly Aid Society." 1950. Concord Free Public Library Special Collections.

Wilinsky, John. "The impact of the railroad on Concord, MA. 1844–1887." Dec. 1, 1975 paper in Concord Free Public Library Special Collections.

"William Munroe's Vision." An exhibition to celebrate the 125th Anniversary of Concord Free Public Library Oct. 1–31, 1998. Prepared by Leslie Wilson and Joyce Woodman of Concord Free Public Library Special Collections.

The Writings of Henry David Thoreau with a biographical sketch by Ralph Waldo Emerson, vol. X. Boston: Houghton, Mifflin & Co., 1893.

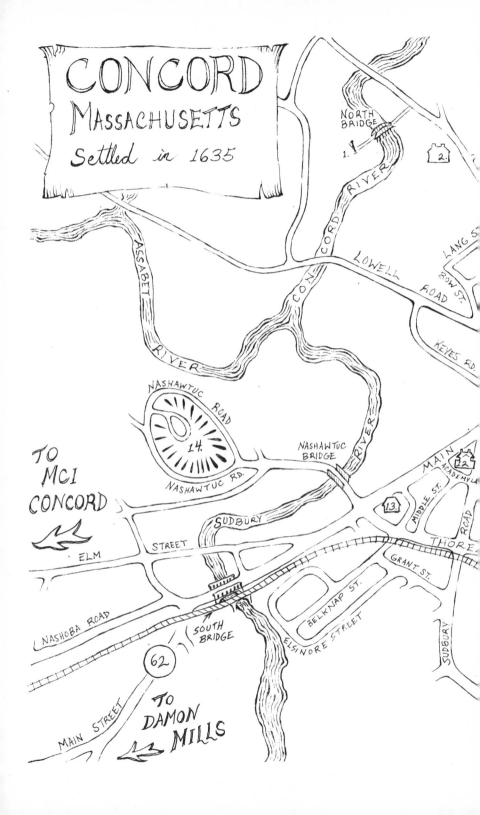